I0012664

Ruby for Beginners, From Fundamentals to Building Full-Stack Applications

The Ultimate Guide to Learning Ruby and Creating Interactive, High-Quality Code

Booker Blunt

Rafael Sanders

Miguel Farmer

Boozman Richard

Contents

How to Scan a Barcode to Get a Repository

1. **Install a QR/Barcode Scanner** – Ensure you have a barcode or QR code scanner app installed on your smartphone or use a built-in scanner in **GitHub, GitLab, or Bitbucket.**

2. **Open the Scanner** – Launch the scanner app and grant necessary camera permissions.

3. **Scan the Barcode** – Align the barcode within the scanning frame. The scanner will automatically detect and process it.

4. **Follow the Link** – The scanned result will display a **URL to the repository**. Tap the link to open it in your web browser or Git client.

5. **Clone the Repository** – Use **Git clone** with the provided URL to download the repository to your local machine.

Chapter 1: Setting Up Your Ruby Environment

1. Introduction

Ruby is a programming language known for its simplicity and readability. Many developers appreciate Ruby for its friendly syntax and expressive code, making it a solid choice for those new to programming as well as experienced coders looking for a clear, concise way to develop applications. In this chapter, we focus on the foundational steps to get you started: installing Ruby on your system, choosing the right development tools and editors, and writing your first Ruby script.

Why Set Up a Proper Environment?

A well-configured development environment is the first step toward a smooth programming experience. Setting up Ruby correctly not only ensures that your code runs efficiently but also minimizes the headaches caused by version mismatches and incompatible libraries. Whether you're developing small scripts for fun or building a full-stack application, having a consistent, reliable setup will let you concentrate on learning and coding without unnecessary distractions.

Key Concepts and Terminology

Before moving forward, it's useful to clarify some key terms that you'll encounter:

- **Interpreter:** Ruby is an interpreted language, meaning your code is executed by a Ruby interpreter rather than compiled into machine language.

- **Version Manager:** Tools like RVM and rbenv help you manage different Ruby versions on the same machine.

- **Integrated Development Environment (IDE):** A software application that provides comprehensive facilities to computer programmers for software development. Common examples include VS Code and RubyMine.

- **Script:** A file containing Ruby code that can be executed to perform a task, such as printing "Hello, World" to the console.

Setting the Tone

The approach in this chapter is hands-on. You will see clear instructions supported by real-life examples that show exactly what happens when you install Ruby, select your tools, and run your first script. Every step is broken down into manageable parts, and visual aids like diagrams and screenshots (placeholders for this text) are integrated to enhance your learning. Even if you've never installed programming software before, the explanations are crafted to guide you confidently through the process.

By the end of this chapter, you should have Ruby installed on your system, be familiar with your development tools, and have run a simple script. With these basic skills, you'll be well-prepared to explore Ruby's capabilities in more advanced applications later in the guide.

2. Core Concepts and Theory

In this section, we dive into the theory behind setting up Ruby. Understanding these concepts will not only help you with the installation but also provide a solid foundation for the coding practices you'll adopt later on.

Understanding Ruby and Its Ecosystem

Ruby is celebrated for its clean syntax and focus on developer productivity. Created in the mid-1990s, Ruby's design emphasizes simplicity and elegance. The language borrows ideas from Perl, Smalltalk, and Lisp, making it a blend of practical programming and a touch of sophistication. When working with Ruby, you're engaging with a language that balances readability with functionality.

The Interpreter and Execution Model

Unlike compiled languages, Ruby code is run by an interpreter. This means you write code in a plain text file, and the Ruby interpreter reads and executes it on the fly. The interpreter converts your human-readable code into actions your computer performs. This model supports quick testing and experimentation, a key reason why many beginners and professionals enjoy using Ruby.

Imagine the interpreter as a translator that converts your instructions into a language the computer understands immediately. This process allows you to test small snippets of code, make adjustments, and see results instantly—a critical feedback loop for learning and development.

Ruby Version Managers: RVM vs. rbenv

Since Ruby evolves over time, different projects may require different Ruby versions. This is where version managers come into play. Two popular options are:

- **RVM (Ruby Version Manager):** Provides a convenient command-line interface to install, manage, and work with multiple Ruby environments. RVM can also manage gem sets, which is useful for keeping project dependencies separate.

- **rbenv:** A lighter alternative that focuses primarily on switching Ruby versions. It integrates well with the shell, making it simple to change your Ruby environment on the fly.

Both tools have their advantages, and your choice may depend on your workflow preferences. For beginners, RVM might seem more straightforward because of its additional features, whereas rbenv offers simplicity if you only need version switching.

The Role of Development Tools and Editors

A proper development environment includes not only the language itself but also the tools you use to write code. Here, editors and IDEs are essential. Popular choices include:

- **Visual Studio Code (VS Code):** Highly customizable with a wide range of extensions for Ruby development. It provides features like syntax highlighting, code snippets, and debugging support.

- **RubyMine:** A dedicated Ruby IDE that offers advanced features such as code navigation, refactoring, and integrated testing tools. It's particularly useful for larger projects.

Think of your development tools as your workshop. Just as a craftsman chooses the right tools to work efficiently, you need a well-configured editor or IDE to write, test, and debug your code effectively.

The Concept of a Script

A script is a file that contains a series of commands for the Ruby interpreter to execute. Scripts can be as simple as printing a message to the console or as complex as a full application. When you run a Ruby script, the interpreter processes the code from top to bottom, performing the actions specified.

Consider a script as a recipe in cooking. Each instruction in the recipe (code line) contributes to the final dish (the executed program). By understanding how scripts work, you gain a clearer picture of the immediate feedback loop between writing code and seeing its effect.

Troubleshooting Installation Issues: Theory Behind the Process

Installation problems often stem from conflicts between system libraries, outdated dependencies, or misconfigured environment variables. Understanding these underlying factors is crucial for troubleshooting. Here are some theoretical points to consider:

- **Dependencies and System Libraries:** Ruby depends on several system libraries to function correctly. A missing or outdated library might cause the installation to fail or the interpreter to behave unexpectedly.

- **Environment Variables:** These are settings that your operating system uses to determine how programs behave. When installing Ruby, ensuring that your PATH variable includes the correct directories is essential.

- **Permissions and Access Rights:** Especially on Unix-based systems, file permissions can affect installation. Running commands with appropriate permissions can resolve many issues.

By grasping these core concepts, you're better prepared to face any challenges during setup and later development.

Summary of Core Theoretical Concepts

To summarize, this section has covered:

- **Ruby's execution model** and why an interpreter-based approach allows rapid development and testing.

- **The role of version managers** like RVM and rbenv in handling multiple Ruby installations, along with their benefits and trade-offs.

- **The importance of development tools and editors** that streamline coding and debugging.

- **The concept of scripts** and their role as executable instructions for the Ruby interpreter.

- **The theory behind troubleshooting installation issues,** including dependencies, environment variables, and permissions.

With this theoretical foundation, you are now ready to move on to the practical aspects of setting up your Ruby environment.

3. Tools and Setup

In this section, we walk through the practical steps to get Ruby running on your machine. We compare different installation methods for various operating systems, provide screenshots and diagrams (indicated as placeholders), and explain each step in detail.

Required Tools and Platforms

Before installing Ruby, you'll need the following:

- **A computer with a supported operating system:** Windows, macOS, or Linux.

- **An internet connection** to download the necessary packages.

- **A terminal or command prompt** to run installation commands.

- **A version manager (optional but recommended):** RVM or rbenv.

- **A code editor or IDE:** VS Code, RubyMine, or another preferred editor.

Installing Ruby on Windows

Step 1: Download the Ruby Installer

1. Visit the Ruby Installer for Windows website.

2. Download the latest stable version. Choose between the 32-bit and 64-bit versions based on your system architecture.

Step 2: Run the Installer

1. Double-click the downloaded installer.

2. Follow the prompts, ensuring that you select the option to add Ruby to your PATH.

3. Complete the installation and open a new command prompt. Type ruby -v to verify that Ruby is installed successfully.

Troubleshooting on Windows

- **Error: "ruby is not recognized as an internal or external command"**
  Verify that the PATH environment variable includes the Ruby installation directory. You can adjust this in the System Properties.

Installing Ruby on macOS

Using Homebrew (Recommended)

Homebrew is a popular package manager for macOS that simplifies software installation.

1. Open Terminal.

2. Install Homebrew (if not already installed) by running the following command:

```bash
/bin/bash -c "$(curl -fsSL
https://raw.githubusercontent.com/Homebrew/install/HEAD/install.sh)"
```

3. Once Homebrew is installed, run:

```
bash

brew install ruby
```

4. After installation, verify with:

```
bash

ruby -v
```

Manual Installation

If you prefer not to use Homebrew, you can download Ruby from the official website and follow the installation instructions provided there.

Troubleshooting on macOS

- **Issue with PATH configuration:**
  After installation via Homebrew, you may need to update your PATH variable. Add the following line to your ~/.bash_profile or ~/.zshrc file:

```
bash

export PATH="/usr/local/opt/ruby/bin:$PATH"
```

- Reload the terminal or run source ~/.zshrc (or source ~/.bash_profile).

Installing Ruby on Linux

Linux users have multiple installation methods. The following instructions use a package manager.

For Ubuntu/Debian

1. Open Terminal.

2. Update your package list:

```
bash

sudo apt-get update
```

3. Install Ruby using:

```
bash
```

```
sudo apt-get install ruby-full
```

4. Verify the installation:

```
bash
```

```
ruby -v
```

For Fedora/CentOS

1. Open Terminal.

2. Install Ruby using:

```
bash
```

```
sudo dnf install ruby
```

or on CentOS:

```
bash
```

```
sudo yum install ruby
```

3. Verify the installation with ruby -v.

Troubleshooting on Linux

- **Missing dependencies:**
  If you encounter dependency issues, consult your package manager's documentation to install any missing libraries.

- **Permission errors:**
  Use sudo where necessary to ensure you have the proper access rights.

Choosing a Version Manager

Although installing Ruby directly through system package managers works well, using a version manager is often more flexible. Here's a brief guide on setting up RVM:

1. Open Terminal.

2. Install RVM with:

```bash
\curl -sSL https://get.rvm.io | bash -s stable
```

3. Follow the on-screen instructions. Once RVM is installed, you can install a specific Ruby version:

```bash
rvm install 3.1.0
```

4. Set the default version:

```bash
rvm use 3.1.0 -default
```

5. Verify with:

```bash
ruby -v
```

Tip: If you prefer rbenv, follow similar steps on its GitHub page.

Setting Up Your Code Editor

Selecting the right editor enhances your development experience. Here are two popular options:

Visual Studio Code (VS Code)

1. Download VS Code from the official website.

2. Install the Ruby extension for syntax highlighting and debugging. Open VS Code, go to the Extensions tab, and search for "Ruby".

3. Configure the settings to match your preferences.

RubyMine

RubyMine is a dedicated IDE for Ruby that offers advanced features. If you prefer an environment tailored for Ruby:

1. Download RubyMine from JetBrains' website.

2. Follow the installation instructions provided on the website.

3. Configure RubyMine to recognize your Ruby installation and set up your project environment.

This section has walked you through the tools required to start working with Ruby. With Ruby installed and your preferred development tools ready, you are prepared to move on to writing your very first script.

4. Hands-on Examples & Projects

Now that your environment is set up, let's write some code. In this section, we will build a series of practical examples that illustrate the basics of Ruby, starting with a "Hello, World" script and moving on to a more engaging project.

Example 1: Your First Ruby Script – "Hello, World"

Writing a "Hello, World" script is a tradition in programming. It serves as an introduction to the syntax and basic execution of Ruby code.

Step-by-Step Walkthrough

1. **Open Your Editor:**
   Launch your code editor (VS Code, RubyMine, or your preferred editor).

2. **Create a New File:**
   Save the file as hello_world.rb.

3. **Write the Code:**

```ruby

# hello_world.rb
# This script prints "Hello, World" to the console.
```

```ruby
puts "Hello, World"
```

4. **Explanation of the Code:**

   o The first two lines are comments that describe what the
     script does.

   o The puts method is used to display text to the console. In
     this case, it prints the string "Hello, World".

5. **Run the Script:**

   o Open your terminal.

   o Navigate to the directory where hello_world.rb is located.

   o Run the command:

```bash
ruby hello_world.rb
```

6. **Observe the Output:**
   The terminal should display:

```
Hello, World
```

Example 2: Building a Simple Calculator

Let's progress to a slightly more complex project—a simple calculator. This
project demonstrates how to get user input, perform basic arithmetic, and
output the result.

Step-by-Step Walkthrough

1. **Create a New File:**
   Save the file as calculator.rb.

2. **Write the Code:**

```ruby
# calculator.rb
```

```ruby
# This simple calculator performs basic arithmetic
operations.

# Function to perform addition
def add(a, b)
  a + b
end

# Function to perform subtraction
def subtract(a, b)
  a - b
end

# Function to perform multiplication
def multiply(a, b)
  a * b
end

# Function to perform division
def divide(a, b)
  if b != 0
    a / b
  else
    "Cannot divide by zero"
  end
end

# Main program execution
puts "Welcome to the Ruby Calculator!"
print "Enter first number: "
num1 = gets.chomp.to_f

print "Enter second number: "
num2 = gets.chomp.to_f

puts "Choose an operation: "
puts "1. Addition"
puts "2. Subtraction"
puts "3. Multiplication"
puts "4. Division"
print "Enter your choice (1/2/3/4): "
choice = gets.chomp

result = case choice
```

```
when "1"
  add(num1, num2)
when "2"
  subtract(num1, num2)
when "3"
  multiply(num1, num2)
when "4"
  divide(num1, num2)
else
  "Invalid operation"
end
```

```
puts "The result is: #{result}"
```

3. **Explanation:**

   o   Functions are defined for each arithmetic operation.

   o   The program prompts the user for two numbers and the desired operation.

   o   A case statement selects the operation based on the user's input.

   o   The result is printed to the console.

4. **Running the Calculator:**

   o   Open your terminal.

   o   Navigate to the directory where calculator.rb is saved.

   o   Execute:

```
bash
```

```
ruby calculator.rb
```

   o   Follow the prompts in the terminal to see the calculation in action.

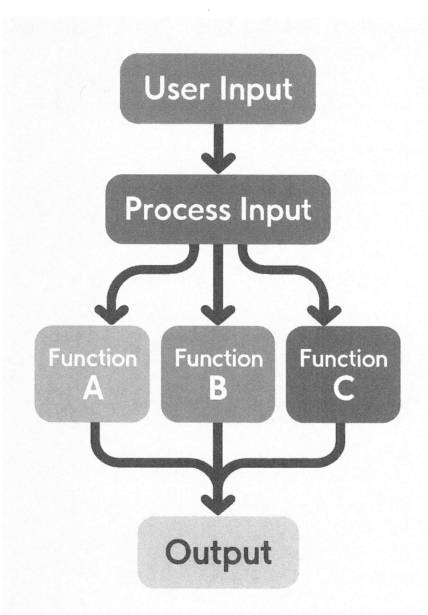

Example 3: A Mini Project – Building a To-Do List Application

For a more engaging project, let's build a simple to-do list application that allows users to add, view, and remove tasks. This project introduces arrays, loops, and conditional statements, offering a comprehensive exercise in basic Ruby.

Step-by-Step Walkthrough

1. **Create a New File:**
    Save the file as todo_list.rb.

2. **Write the Code:**

```ruby
# todo_list.rb
# This script manages a simple to-do list

# Initialize an empty list to store tasks
todo_list = []

# Method to display the to-do list
def display_list(list)
  puts "\nYour To-Do List:"
  list.each_with_index do |task, index|
    puts "#{index + 1}. #{task}"
  end
  puts "\n"
end

loop do
  puts "To-Do List Menu:"
  puts "1. Add a task"
  puts "2. Remove a task"
  puts "3. View tasks"
  puts "4. Exit"
  print "Choose an option (1-4): "
  option = gets.chomp

  case option
  when "1"
    print "Enter a new task: "
```

```ruby
      task = gets.chomp
      todo_list << task
      puts "Task added successfully!"
    when "2"
      if todo_list.empty?
        puts "Your list is empty. Nothing to remove."
      else
        display_list(todo_list)
        print "Enter the task number to remove: "
        index = gets.chomp.to_i - 1
        if index >= 0 && index < todo_list.size
          removed = todo_list.delete_at(index)
          puts "Removed task: #{removed}"
        else
          puts "Invalid task number."
        end
      end
    when "3"
      if todo_list.empty?
        puts "Your to-do list is currently empty."
      else
        display_list(todo_list)
      end
    when "4"
      puts "Exiting the To-Do List Application.
Goodbye!"
      break
    else
      puts "Invalid option. Please choose between 1 and
4."
    end
end
```

3. **Explanation:**

   o An array named todo_list stores tasks.

   o The display_list method prints the current tasks with numbering.

   o A loop presents a menu for the user to add, remove, or view tasks.

  o   The case statement handles user input, ensuring a clear
      flow of operations.

4.   **Running the To-Do List Application:**

  o   Open your terminal.

  o   Navigate to the directory where todo_list.rb is saved.

  o   Run the command:

```bash
ruby todo_list.rb
```

  o   Follow the on-screen prompts to interact with your to-do
      list.

Code Quality and Best Practices

Each example in this section emphasizes readability and simplicity. The
code is well-commented to ensure that every function and command is
understandable. In a production environment, these practices help
maintain and scale applications with ease. For every script:

• **Comments** provide context.

• **Clean indentation** ensures the structure is visible.

• **Descriptive function names** help clarify purpose.

Combining Projects for a Full-Fledged Application

After practicing with smaller projects like "Hello, World," a calculator,
and a to-do list, consider combining these elements. For instance, you
might extend the to-do list by adding features like task deadlines or
categorization. By gradually building up complexity, you refine your skills
without feeling overwhelmed.

Imagine a scenario where your to-do list app interacts with a database to
persist tasks between sessions. While this goes beyond the basics, the
current projects lay the groundwork for more advanced implementations.
Experiment with different features, and document any changes you make.

Collaborative Coding and Version Control

An essential part of any project is version control. Using tools like Git can help you manage changes in your code. Here's a quick overview:

1. **Initialize a Git Repository:**

```bash
git init
```

2. **Add Files and Commit:**

```bash
git add .
git commit -m "Initial commit: Add basic to-do list
application"
```

3. **Branching for New Features:**
   Create a new branch for experimental features, ensuring your main branch remains stable.

Hands-on Project Recap

This hands-on section is designed to bridge theory with practice. As you work through these examples:

- You'll see how user input, control structures, and data structures form the backbone of Ruby programming.

- The projects demonstrate real-world scenarios like managing tasks or performing calculations, which can be adapted for larger applications.

- Each project builds on the previous ones, encouraging you to experiment and extend functionalities.

5. Advanced Techniques & Optimization

Now that you have built and experimented with basic Ruby scripts and small applications, this section explores advanced techniques for managing and optimizing your Ruby environment.

Optimizing Ruby Installations

After you have set up Ruby using a package manager or version manager, there are several tweaks you can make for performance and reliability. For example, ensuring that your PATH variables are correctly configured can lead to faster command executions. You might also consider the following:

- **Managing Multiple Versions:**
  Use RVM or rbenv to switch between Ruby versions effortlessly. For instance, if you work on multiple projects with different requirements, these tools allow you to isolate dependencies and avoid conflicts.

- **Gem Management:**
  RubyGems is the package manager for Ruby libraries (gems). Keeping your gems up to date ensures that you benefit from performance improvements and security fixes. Regularly run:

```bash

gem update
```

Benchmarking:
```
Utilize benchmarking libraries to measure performance
of critical sections of your code. A simple
benchmarking example in Ruby is:
```
```ruby

require 'benchmark'

time = Benchmark.measure do
  # Your code block
  1000.times { "Ruby".reverse }
end
```

puts time

Best Practices for Code Structure and Performance

Well-organized code not only runs faster but is easier to maintain and extend. Some best practices include:

- **Modular Design:**
  Break your code into reusable methods and classes.

- **DRY Principle (Don't Repeat Yourself):**
  Reuse code rather than duplicating functionality.

- **Testing and Profiling:**
  Use testing frameworks and profiling tools to identify bottlenecks
  in your code.

Advanced Code Examples

Let's examine some advanced snippets that highlight optimization and
clean coding techniques.

Example: Optimizing a Data Processing Task

Consider a scenario where you need to process a large array of numbers.
Instead of processing each element with a complex loop, Ruby's built-in
methods can perform tasks more efficiently.

```ruby

# Optimized code for summing an array of numbers

numbers = (1..1000000).to_a

# Using built-in method for efficiency
sum = numbers.inject(:+)
puts "The sum is: #{sum}"
```

Explanation:
Using inject is more efficient and readable than manually iterating over
each element with a loop. This code snippet illustrates how Ruby's
enumerable methods can simplify tasks.

Example: Memoization for Performance

Memoization is a technique to store results of expensive function calls and
reuse them when the same inputs occur again.

```ruby

# A simple example of memoization in Ruby
def fibonacci(n, memo = {})
  return n if n < 2
```

```
  memo[n] ||= fibonacci(n - 1, memo) + fibonacci(n -
2, memo)
end
```

puts fibonacci(35)

Explanation:
Without memoization, calculating Fibonacci numbers recursively would
be extremely slow. This snippet shows how caching intermediate results
dramatically improves performance.

Advanced Tooling

For professional developers, integrating advanced tools like debuggers and
profilers can improve your workflow. Tools such as:

- **Byebug:** A debugger for Ruby that lets you step through your
  code.

- **Rack Mini Profiler:** Useful for profiling web applications.

These tools provide insights into your application's performance, helping
you identify and optimize critical sections of your code.

Visualizing Optimization

Flowcharts and diagrams can help illustrate complex optimizations. For
example, a flowchart showing the decision-making process in a memoized
function can clarify how repeated calculations are avoided.

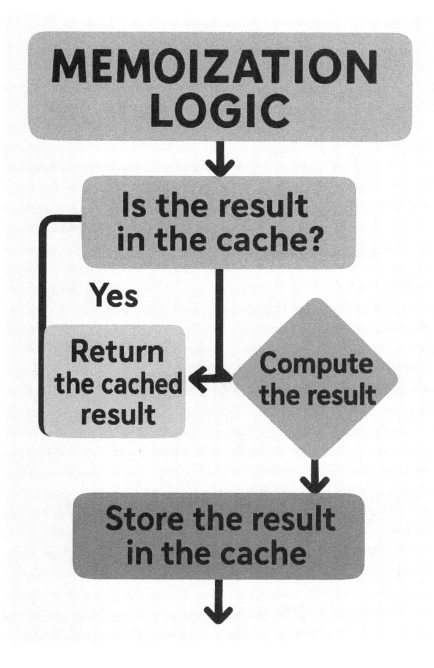

Strategies for Maintaining a Clean Codebase

As your projects grow, maintaining a clean codebase is essential. Some strategies include:

- **Regular Code Reviews:**
  Peer reviews help catch inefficiencies and maintain coding standards.

- **Automated Testing:**
  Use tools like RSpec to write tests that ensure your code behaves as expected.

- **Continuous Integration:**
  Implement CI tools to automate testing and deployment.

Advanced Techniques Recap

This section has examined various techniques and strategies to optimize your Ruby environment and code. By applying these advanced concepts, you enhance both performance and maintainability, making it easier to scale your projects over time.

---

6. Troubleshooting and Problem-Solving

Even with a clear guide, challenges can arise. This section provides common troubleshooting scenarios and offers step-by-step solutions to overcome them.

Common Installation Issues

Issue: Ruby Command Not Found

- **Symptoms:**
  Running ruby -v returns an error message stating that Ruby is not recognized.

- **Potential Causes:**

  o   Ruby was not added to the PATH.

    o   The installation did not complete successfully.

- **Solution:**

    o   Verify the installation directory.

    o   On Windows, ensure the Ruby installation path is included in the PATH environment variable. On macOS or Linux, check your shell configuration files (e.g., ~/.bash_profile or ~/.zshrc) for the correct export commands.

    o   Restart your terminal after making changes.

Issue: Dependency Conflicts

- **Symptoms:**
  Errors indicating that certain gems or libraries are missing.

- **Potential Causes:**

    o   Incompatible gem versions.

    o   Missing system libraries required by Ruby.

- **Solution:**

    o   Use a version manager (RVM/rbenv) to isolate your environment.

    o   Check the gem documentation for dependencies.

    o   Use package managers like Homebrew or apt-get to install missing libraries.

Debugging Code Errors

When writing Ruby scripts, errors and exceptions can occur. Here's a systematic approach to debugging:

1. **Read the Error Message Carefully:**
   Ruby error messages typically indicate the file and line number where the problem occurred.

2. **Use a Debugger:**
   Insert byebug into your code and run your script to step through execution.

3. **Print Debug Information:**
   Use puts statements to output variable values at critical points in your script.

4. **Consult the Documentation:**
   Look up error messages in the Ruby documentation or community forums for guidance.

Before-and-After Examples

Let's look at a before-and-after scenario with code improvements:

Before: Unclear Error Handling

```ruby
def divide(a, b)
  a / b
end

puts divide(10, 0)
```

Problem:
Dividing by zero results in an error without explanation.

After: Clear Error Handling

```ruby
def divide(a, b)
  if b == 0
  "Division by zero is not allowed."

  else
    a / b
  end
end

puts divide(10, 0)
```

Explanation:
The updated version checks for a zero divisor and returns a friendly message instead of crashing the program.

Handling Installation-Specific Challenges

Some challenges are specific to the installation process. For example:

- **Version Manager Issues:**
  If switching Ruby versions with RVM or rbenv doesn't work as expected, ensure that your terminal is sourcing the correct configuration file. Revisit the installation instructions and verify that all necessary commands have been executed.

- **Permissions Errors:**
  On Unix-based systems, installation commands may require sudo privileges. However, avoid using sudo with version managers to prevent permission conflicts.

Debugging Tools and Resources

Leverage the following tools and resources when troubleshooting:

- **Ruby Documentation:**
  The official Ruby documentation provides insights into error messages and best practices.

- **Community Forums:**
  Websites such as Stack Overflow offer community support where you can search for or ask questions about common issues.

- **Local Logs:**
  Some IDEs, like RubyMine, include integrated consoles and logs that track runtime errors and warnings.

Final Tips for Effective Troubleshooting

- **Stay Calm and Systematic:**
  Document each step you take to resolve an issue. This habit will make it easier to pinpoint recurring problems.

- **Regularly Update Your Tools:**
  Keeping Ruby, gems, and version managers up to date reduces the chance of encountering compatibility issues.

- **Learn from Each Error:**
  Every error encountered is an opportunity to deepen your
  understanding of Ruby and its environment.

---

7. Conclusion & Next Steps

In this chapter, you learned how to set up your Ruby environment—a
critical first step in your programming journey. We covered the installation
process for various operating systems, explored the role of version
managers and development tools, and guided you through writing your
first scripts. Each section provided practical, real-world examples to ensure
you not only understand the concepts but can apply them immediately.

Key Takeaways

- **Ruby Installation:**
  You are now familiar with installing Ruby on Windows, macOS,
  and Linux. Whether using direct installers or package managers,
  you learned how to verify and troubleshoot your installation.

- **Development Tools:**
  By choosing an appropriate code editor or IDE, you set the stage
  for efficient development. Tools like VS Code and RubyMine are
  now at your fingertips.

- **First Script:**
  Writing a "Hello, World" script, a simple calculator, and a to-do
  list application has introduced you to the fundamental building
  blocks of Ruby programming.

- **Advanced Techniques:**
  Techniques such as memoization, efficient code structure, and
  using advanced debugging tools were discussed to prepare you for
  more complex projects.

- **Troubleshooting:**
  Common pitfalls and error messages were addressed with
  practical solutions, ensuring that you can overcome challenges as
  you code.

What's Next?

Now that your environment is set up and you have written several scripts, consider the following steps to continue your Ruby journey:

- **Practice:**
  Build more small projects. Experiment with adding new features to the projects introduced in this chapter.

- **Explore:**
  Read additional documentation and online tutorials that cover Ruby's advanced features. Look into frameworks like Ruby on Rails if you're interested in web development.

- **Join the Community:**
  Engage with other Ruby developers through forums, local meetups, and online communities. Learning from others' experiences will accelerate your progress.

- **Use Version Control:**
  If you haven't already, start using Git to track your projects. This will not only help you manage your code but also prepare you for collaborative work.

Additional Resources

Here are some recommended resources to further your learning:

- **Official Ruby Website:**
  Offers tutorials, documentation, and news on the latest Ruby updates.

- **RubyGems:**
  Explore libraries and tools that can extend your Ruby applications.

- **Community Forums:**
  Stack Overflow, Reddit's r/ruby, and local meetup groups are great places to ask questions and share ideas.

Final Thoughts

Setting up your development environment correctly is a foundation for all the exciting projects you'll build in Ruby. With a stable environment, effective tools, and hands-on projects under your belt, you're well-equipped to explore Ruby's capabilities further. Take your time to experiment, ask questions, and practice what you have learned.

Remember, every programmer encounters errors and obstacles. The key is to approach these challenges with a systematic mindset, using the resources and techniques outlined in this chapter. As you continue, you will find that each new project enhances your understanding and confidence in your coding skills.

By now, you should have a clear picture of how to set up Ruby, choose your tools, and write basic scripts. The journey ahead involves expanding your knowledge with more complex applications, integrating advanced techniques, and, most importantly, enjoying the process of learning and coding in Ruby.

Chapter 2: Ruby Basics

1. Introduction

Ruby is renowned for its readability and simplicity, making it an excellent language for newcomers and experienced developers alike. In this chapter, we explore the fundamental aspects of Ruby programming, starting with its syntax and basic constructs, moving through control structures that govern program flow, and finally taking a look at Ruby's built-in data structures. The goal is to provide you with a solid foundation that not only explains how Ruby works but also why it's structured the way it is.

Imagine learning Ruby as if you were learning a new spoken language. Every language has its grammar rules, vocabulary, and idioms. In Ruby, the "grammar" is the syntax, the "vocabulary" includes keywords, operators, and constructs like variables, strings, and numbers, while "idioms" are the common patterns you'll use in everyday coding. Whether you're automating tasks, building web applications, or exploring programming as a hobby, understanding these basics is essential.

Significance of Ruby's Basics

Understanding Ruby's basic constructs is not just about learning how to write code; it's about building a mental model of how Ruby "thinks." This chapter explains the reasoning behind Ruby's design, emphasizing clarity and expressiveness. You'll learn how the language's natural, almost conversational syntax can reduce the mental load when reading and writing code. This clarity makes debugging and extending your programs much more approachable.

Key Concepts and Terminology

Throughout this chapter, you'll encounter several key terms:

- **Variable:** A placeholder for storing data, much like a container for values.

- **String:** A sequence of characters used to represent text.

- **Number:** Numeric values which can be integers or floating-point numbers.

- **Operator:** Symbols that perform operations on variables and values (e.g., +, -, *, /).

- **Conditional Statements:** Structures that allow your program to make decisions based on certain conditions.

- **Loop:** A control structure that repeats a block of code until a specified condition is met.

- **Array and Hash:** Fundamental data structures used to organize collections of values.

These terms form the building blocks of Ruby programming. By the end of this chapter, you will not only be comfortable with the syntax but also understand how to leverage Ruby's control structures and data types to solve real-world problems.

Setting the Tone

The tone of this chapter is both professional and approachable. You'll find that technical jargon is explained in everyday language, with analogies and examples that relate to common experiences. For instance, think of variables as labeled boxes where you store ingredients for a recipe. Just as you might choose different boxes for flour, sugar, or spices, you choose variables to hold different types of data. This familiar analogy makes it easier to understand how Ruby handles information.

Throughout the chapter, we encourage you to experiment with the provided code examples. Don't hesitate to modify them and see what happens—this hands-on approach is one of the best ways to solidify your learning. As you progress, keep in mind that every small step builds your programming muscle, preparing you for more advanced topics later on.

By the end of this chapter, you'll have a clear understanding of Ruby's syntax, the mechanics behind control structures, and how to work with arrays, hashes, and other data types. This foundational knowledge will serve as the stepping stone to more complex projects and help you become a more confident Ruby developer.

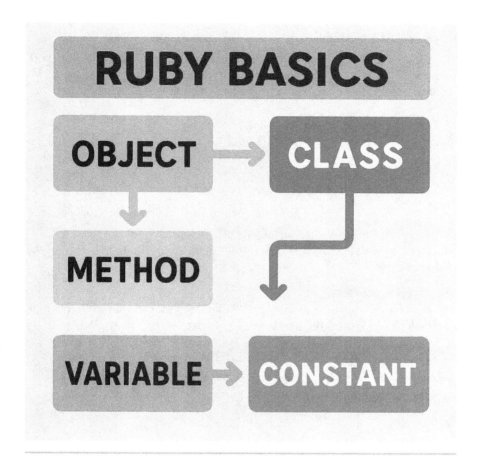

2. Core Concepts and Theory

In this section, we dive deep into the core concepts that define Ruby's basic structure. We'll explore the language's syntax, break down its fundamental constructs, and explain how to control the flow of your programs.

2.1 Syntax and Basic Constructs

Ruby's syntax is designed to be natural and intuitive. The language minimizes boilerplate code and encourages a style that reads almost like plain English. Let's explore the essential elements:

2.1.1 Variables

Variables are the foundation of any programming language. In Ruby, you simply assign a value to a name, and that name becomes your variable. For example:

ruby

```
# Assigning a string to a variable
greeting = "Hello, world!"

# Assigning a number to a variable
age = 25
```

Variables in Ruby are dynamically typed, meaning you don't need to declare a type explicitly. The interpreter determines the type based on the value assigned.

Real-World Analogy:
Think of a variable as a jar labeled "Cookies." You can fill it with any type of cookies (data), and the label doesn't change the cookie itself.

2.1.2 Strings and Numbers

Ruby provides straightforward ways to work with strings (text) and numbers. Strings are defined by enclosing text within quotes:

ruby

```
message = "Welcome to Ruby Basics!"
```
Numbers can be integers or floating-point values:

ruby

```
integer_example = 42
float_example = 3.14159
```
You can perform arithmetic operations using basic operators:

ruby

```
sum = 5 + 3        # => 8
difference = 10 - 2  # => 8
product = 4 * 3   # => 12
quotient = 12 / 3   # => 4
```

2.1.3 Comments

Comments are lines in your code that the interpreter ignores. They're used to explain what the code is doing, making it easier to understand later. Ruby supports single-line and multi-line comments:

```ruby

# This is a single-line comment

=begin
This is a
multi-line comment
=end
```

Using comments effectively helps both you and others to understand the logic behind your code.

2.2 Control Structures and Flow

Control structures dictate the flow of your program. They allow your code to make decisions and repeat actions, which is essential for any dynamic application.

2.2.1 Conditional Statements

Conditional statements enable your program to take different paths based on specific conditions. The most common structure is the if statement:

```ruby

temperature = 75

if temperature > 80
  puts "It's hot outside!"
elsif temperature < 60
  puts "It's cool outside!"
else
  puts "The weather is moderate."
end
```

In this example, the program checks the temperature and prints a message based on its value. The use of elsif and else ensures that all possibilities are covered.

Everyday Decision Analogy:
Imagine deciding what to wear based on the weather. If it's hot, you choose shorts; if it's cold, you opt for a jacket; otherwise, you select something in between.

2.2.2 Looping Constructs

Loops are essential when you need to repeat a block of code multiple times. Ruby provides several types of loops, including while, until, and iterators such as each.

While Loop:

```ruby
counter = 1

while counter <= 5
  puts "Counter is at #{counter}"
  counter += 1
end
```

This loop runs as long as the condition is true. In this case, it prints the counter's value until it exceeds 5.

Until Loop:

```ruby
counter = 1

until counter > 5
  puts "Counter is at #{counter}"
  counter += 1
end
```

The until loop does the opposite of while—it runs until the condition becomes true.

Iterator:

```ruby
[1, 2, 3, 4, 5].each do |number|
  puts "Number is: #{number}"
end
```

Using iterators like each is idiomatic in Ruby and is preferred for traversing arrays and collections.

2.2.3 Case Statements

Case statements are a compact alternative to multiple if/elsif conditions, making your code more readable when dealing with numerous possibilities:

```ruby

day = "Tuesday"

message = case day
          when "Monday"
            "Start of the workweek!"
          when "Friday"
            "Almost the weekend!"
          else
            "Just another day."
          end
```

puts message

This structure is similar to a switch-case statement in other languages and can simplify your code when evaluating a single variable against multiple values.

2.3 Working with Data Structures

Ruby provides powerful built-in data structures that help you manage and manipulate collections of data. The most common data structures include arrays and hashes.

2.3.1 Arrays

Arrays are ordered lists of elements. They are defined using square brackets:

```ruby

fruits = ["apple", "banana", "cherry"]
```
You can access elements using their index (starting at 0):

```ruby
```

```ruby
first_fruit = fruits[0]   # => "apple"
```

Arrays in Ruby come with a host of useful methods for iteration, filtering, and transformation. For example:

```ruby
```

```ruby
# Adding an element
fruits << "date"

# Iterating through each element
fruits.each do |fruit|
  puts "I like #{fruit}"
end
```

Everyday Analogy:

Consider an array as a grocery list. Each item on the list has a specific order, and you can add, remove, or modify items as needed.

2.3.2 Hashes

Hashes are collections of key-value pairs, similar to dictionaries in other programming languages. They are defined using curly braces:

```ruby
```

```ruby
person = { name: "Alice", age: 30, occupation:
"Developer" }
```

You can access values by their corresponding keys:

```ruby
```

```ruby
puts person[:name]   # => "Alice"
```

Hashes are particularly useful for storing related data where each piece of information has a unique identifier.

2.3.3 Other Data Structures

Ruby also supports other data types, such as ranges and sets. Ranges are used to represent sequences of values:

```ruby
```

```ruby
numbers = (1..10).to_a   # Converts the range to an
array
```

Sets, provided by the standard library, are collections of unique items. They are ideal for scenarios where duplicate entries are not desired.

```ruby
require 'set'

unique_numbers = Set.new([1, 2, 3, 3, 4])
puts unique_numbers.to_a   # => [1, 2, 3, 4]
```

Recap of Core Theoretical Concepts

At this point, you should understand:

- **Ruby Syntax:** Variables, strings, numbers, and operators form the backbone of Ruby programming.

- **Control Structures:** Conditionals (if/elsif/else), loops (while, until, each), and case statements provide flow control.

- **Data Structures:** Arrays, hashes, ranges, and sets help you store and manipulate data effectively.

Each of these concepts works together to create the building blocks for more advanced programming. With this foundation, you're now ready to set up your coding environment and start putting these ideas into practice.

---

3. Tools and Setup

Before diving into more complex projects, it's important to ensure you have the right tools to write and test your Ruby code. This section covers the software and platforms necessary for Ruby development, along with step-by-step instructions for setting up your environment.

3.1 Required Tools and Platforms

For this chapter, you will need:

- **Ruby Interpreter:** Ensure you have Ruby installed on your machine. Use the installation guide from Chapter 1 if needed.

- **Text Editor or IDE:** Choose an editor such as Visual Studio Code (VS Code) or RubyMine. Both provide syntax highlighting, code completion, and debugging support.

- **Terminal/Command Prompt:** A place to run your Ruby scripts.

- **Version Control System (Optional):** Git can help you manage your code versions and collaborate on projects.

3.2 Installing and Configuring Your Editor

Visual Studio Code (VS Code)

1. **Download and Install:**
   Visit the VS Code website and download the installer for your operating system. Follow the on-screen instructions to install.

2. **Install Ruby Extensions:**
   Open VS Code and navigate to the Extensions view. Search for "Ruby" and install a popular Ruby extension that supports syntax highlighting and debugging.

3. **Configure Settings:**
   Customize your settings to improve readability. For instance, adjust font size, tab spacing, and enable linting if desired.

RubyMine

1. **Download and Install:**
   RubyMine, developed by JetBrains, is a dedicated IDE for Ruby. Download it from the RubyMine website and install it.

2. **Initial Setup:**
   Launch RubyMine and configure it to locate your Ruby installation. This step ensures that RubyMine can run your scripts and provide debugging tools.

3.3 Setting Up Your Terminal

Depending on your operating system, you might use different terminal applications:

- **macOS/Linux:** The built-in Terminal application.

- **Windows:** Command Prompt or PowerShell. Alternatively, you can install Git Bash for a Unix-like terminal experience.

Verify that Ruby is correctly installed by opening your terminal and typing:

```
bash
```

```
ruby -v
```
This command should output your installed Ruby version.

3.4 Creating Your First Ruby File

Now that you have your environment set up, it's time to create a Ruby file and run a simple script.

1. **Open Your Editor:**
   Create a new file and name it basics.rb.

2. **Write a Simple Code Snippet:**
   For example, add the following code to print a welcome message:

```ruby
# basics.rb
# This script demonstrates basic Ruby syntax and
constructs.

greeting = "Welcome to Ruby Basics!"
puts greeting
```

3. **Run the Script:**
   Open your terminal, navigate to the file's directory, and run:

```bash
ruby basics.rb
```
The terminal should display the greeting message.

3.5 Summary of Tools and Setup

This section has walked you through the essential tools and setup required for Ruby development:

- Installation of the Ruby interpreter.

- Setting up your preferred text editor or IDE.

- Configuring your terminal and verifying Ruby installation.

- Creating and running a basic Ruby file.

By ensuring your tools are configured correctly, you pave the way for smooth, efficient coding as you dive into more complex Ruby examples.

4. Hands-on Examples & Projects

Now that the theoretical foundation and tools are in place, it's time to apply what you've learned with hands-on projects. In this section, you'll work through several practical examples, starting with simple code snippets and progressing to small projects that reinforce Ruby basics.

4.1 Example 1: Getting Started with Basic Syntax

Project: "Hello, Ruby!"

This introductory project reinforces variable assignment, string manipulation, and output methods.

1. **Create a File:**
   Name it hello_ruby.rb.

2. **Write the Code:**

```ruby

# hello_ruby.rb
# A simple script to welcome you to Ruby.

welcome_message = "Hello, Ruby!"
puts welcome_message
```

3. **Run the Script:**
   Open your terminal, navigate to the directory, and execute:

```bash

ruby hello_ruby.rb
```

4. **Expected Output:**
   The terminal displays:

```
Hello, Ruby!
```

Exercise:
Change the message to include your name. Save and run the script again.

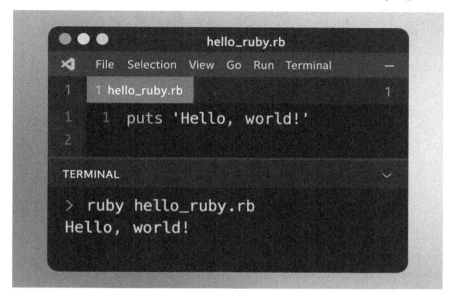

4.2 Example 2: Exploring Variables, Strings, and Numbers

Project: "Personalized Greeting"

This example demonstrates the use of variables with different data types and simple arithmetic operations.

1. **Create a File:**
   Name it personal_greeting.rb.

2. **Write the Code:**

```ruby
# personal_greeting.rb
# This script combines strings and numbers to create
a personalized greeting.

name = "Alex"
```

```
age = 28
greeting = "Hello, #{name}! Next year, you'll be
#{age + 1} years old."
puts greeting
```

3. **Explanation:**

   o String interpolation (#{}) inserts variable values directly into strings.

   o A simple arithmetic operation is performed within the interpolation.

4. **Run the Script:**
   Execute the file in your terminal:

5.

```bash
ruby personal_greeting.rb
```

6. **Expected Output:**

```vbnet
Hello, Alex! Next year, you'll be 29 years old.
```
Exercise:
Modify the script to include a favorite hobby in the greeting.

4.3 Example 3: Control Structures in Action

Project: "Weather Decision Helper"

This project illustrates the use of conditional statements to make decisions based on input values.

1. **Create a File:**
   Name it weather_helper.rb.

2. **Write the Code:**

```ruby
# weather_helper.rb
# This script gives advice based on the temperature
input.
```

```
print "Enter the current temperature (in °F): "
temperature = gets.chomp.to_i

if temperature > 80
  puts "It's quite warm outside. Stay hydrated!"
elsif temperature < 60
  puts "It might be chilly. Consider wearing a
jacket."
else
  puts "The weather is moderate. Enjoy your day!"
end
```

3. **Explanation:**

   o   The gets.chomp.to_i converts user input into an integer.

   o   Conditional statements (if, elsif, else) direct the flow based on the temperature value.

4. **Run the Script:**
   Test the script by entering different temperature values.

Exercise:
Add another condition for exactly 75°F and print a specific message.

4.4 Example 4: Iteration with Loops

Project: "Countdown Timer"

This example uses a loop to create a countdown sequence.

1. **Create a File:**
   Name it countdown.rb.

```
Write the Code:
ruby

# countdown.rb
# This script performs a countdown from 10 to 1.

number = 10
while number > 0
  puts "Countdown: #{number}"
  number -= 1
end
```

```
puts "Blast off!"
```

2. **Explanation:**

   o   The while loop repeats until the condition is false.

   o   The counter variable is decremented each iteration.

3. **Run the Script:**
   Execute in the terminal:

```bash
```

```
ruby countdown.rb
```
Exercise:
Modify the script to count down by 2's instead of 1's.

4.5 Example 5: Working with Arrays and Hashes

Project: "Student Roster Manager"

This project integrates arrays and hashes to manage a list of students and their details.

1. **Create a File:**
   Name it student_roster.rb.

2. **Write the Code:**

```ruby
```

```ruby
# student_roster.rb
# This script manages a simple student roster using
arrays and hashes.

# Initialize an array of student hashes
students = [
  { name: "Alice", grade: "A" },
  { name: "Bob", grade: "B" },
  { name: "Charlie", grade: "C" }
]

# Display the roster
puts "Student Roster:"
students.each_with_index do |student, index|
```

```
   puts "#{index + 1}. Name: #{student[:name]}, Grade:
#{student[:grade]}"
end

# Add a new student
print "Enter a new student's name: "
new_name = gets.chomp
print "Enter the new student's grade: "
new_grade = gets.chomp

students << { name: new_name, grade: new_grade }
puts "Updated Roster:"
students.each_with_index do |student, index|
   puts "#{index + 1}. Name: #{student[:name]}, Grade:
#{student[:grade]}"
end
```

3. **Explanation:**

   o Arrays store multiple elements, and each student is
     represented by a hash.

   o The script uses iteration to display and update the roster.

4. **Run the Script:**
   Execute and follow the prompts to add a new student.

Exercise:
Sort the student roster alphabetically by name before displaying it.

4.6 Combining Concepts into a Mini-Project

Project: "Interactive Quiz Application"

Now, let's combine variables, control structures, loops, and data structures
to build an interactive quiz application.

1. **Create a File:**
   Name it quiz_app.rb.

2. **Write the Code:**

```ruby

# quiz_app.rb
```

```ruby
# An interactive quiz application that tests your
knowledge.

# Define a set of quiz questions in an array of
hashes
quiz = [
  { question: "What is the capital of France?",
answer: "Paris" },
  { question: "What is 5 multiplied by 6?", answer:
"30" },
  { question: "What programming language is known for
its readability?", answer: "Ruby" }
]

score = 0

puts "Welcome to the Ruby Quiz!"
quiz.each_with_index do |item, index|
  puts "\nQuestion #{index + 1}: #{item[:question]}"
  print "Your answer: "
  user_answer = gets.chomp.strip

  if user_answer.casecmp(item[:answer]) == 0
    puts "Correct!"
    score += 1
  else
    puts "Incorrect. The correct answer is
#{item[:answer]}."
  end
end

puts "\nYour final score is #{score} out of
#{quiz.length}."
```

3. **Explanation:**

   o   The quiz is stored as an array of hashes.

   o   A loop iterates through each question, comparing the user's answer to the correct one.

   o   Case-insensitive comparison ensures fairness.

4. **Run the Script:**
   Test the quiz application in your terminal.

Exercise:
Expand the quiz by adding more questions or implementing a timer for each question.

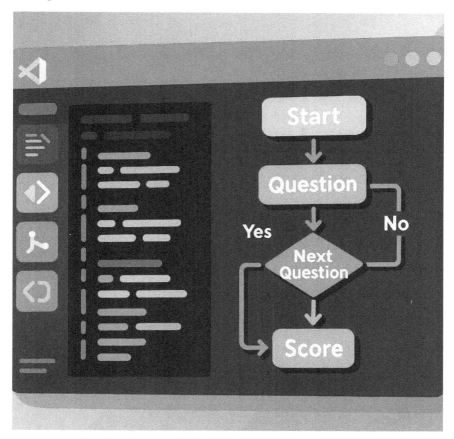

4.7 Project Recap and Reflection

In these hands-on examples, you have:

- Explored Ruby's basic syntax through simple scripts.

- Applied control structures to build dynamic programs.

- Worked with arrays and hashes to manage data collections.

- Combined multiple concepts to build an interactive quiz.

These projects are designed to reinforce the theoretical concepts discussed earlier, offering practical applications that you can adapt for your own needs.

5. Advanced Techniques & Optimization

As you become comfortable with Ruby's basics, it's beneficial to explore some advanced techniques that can optimize your code and enhance your development process. This section introduces strategies that experienced developers use to write cleaner, more efficient Ruby code.

5.1 Code Refactoring and Clean Code Practices

Over time, you'll learn that not all code is created equal. Refactoring is the process of improving code structure without altering its external behavior. In Ruby, this might mean extracting repeated code into reusable methods, improving variable names, or simplifying complex conditionals.

Example: Refactoring a Repetitive Conditional

Consider a script that prints a greeting based on the time of day:

```ruby

# Before refactoring
time = Time.now.hour

if time < 12
  puts "Good morning!"
elsif time >= 12 && time < 18
  puts "Good afternoon!"
else
  puts "Good evening!"
end
```

Refactor by extracting the greeting logic into a method:

```ruby

def greeting_for(time)
```

```
if time < 12
  "Good morning!"
elsif time < 18
  "Good afternoon!"
else
  "Good evening!"
end
end
```

```
puts greeting_for(Time.now.hour)
```
This refactoring enhances clarity and makes the code easier to maintain.

5.2 Optimizing Data Structure Operations

Ruby's enumerable methods like map, select, and inject are powerful tools that allow you to perform complex operations in a concise manner. Consider the task of summing values in an array:

```ruby

numbers = [10, 20, 30, 40, 50]

# Using inject for summing values
total = numbers.inject(0) { |sum, number| sum +
number }
puts "Total: #{total}"
```
Using built-in methods not only improves readability but also leverages Ruby's optimized internal implementations.

5.3 Advanced Iterators and Enumerators

Beyond simple loops, Ruby provides advanced iteration techniques that can improve the performance of your code. Learn how to chain enumerators to filter, map, and reduce data in a single statement:

```ruby

numbers = (1..100).to_a

# Filter even numbers and then sum them
even_sum = numbers.select { |n| n.even? }.inject(0,
:+)
puts "Sum of even numbers: #{even_sum}"
```

This one-liner is both concise and expressive, illustrating Ruby's strength in data processing.

5.4 Memoization Techniques

Memoization is a strategy used to cache the results of expensive method calls and reuse them when needed. This is particularly useful for recursive methods or calculations that are performed repeatedly.

```ruby
def factorial(n, memo = {})
  return 1 if n <= 1
  memo[n] ||= n * factorial(n - 1, memo)
end

puts factorial(10)
```

Memoization helps reduce redundant computations and speeds up execution significantly.

5.5 Visualizing Advanced Concepts

Visual aids like flowcharts and diagrams are invaluable when tackling advanced concepts. Consider a flowchart that explains the process of memoization in recursive functions. Such diagrams can clarify how caching works and why it improves performance.

5.6 Best Practices for Optimization

To write truly efficient Ruby code, consider the following best practices:

- **Modular Design:** Break your code into smaller, reusable methods and classes.

- **DRY (Don't Repeat Yourself):** Avoid duplication by reusing code wherever possible.

- **Profiling and Benchmarking:** Use libraries such as benchmark to measure the performance of critical code sections.

Example: Benchmarking Code

```ruby
require 'benchmark'
```

```
time = Benchmark.measure do
  100_000.times { "Ruby".reverse }
end
```

```
puts "Time taken: #{time.real} seconds"
```
Benchmarking helps you identify performance bottlenecks and optimize accordingly.

5.7 Advanced Techniques Recap

In this section, we've explored several advanced techniques that can transform your Ruby code from functional to exceptional:

- Refactoring for readability and maintainability.

- Leveraging Ruby's enumerable methods for efficient data processing.

- Using memoization to optimize recursive calculations.

- Incorporating best practices for performance and modular design.

These strategies are invaluable as you tackle larger projects and aim for clean, efficient code.

---

6. Troubleshooting and Problem-Solving

Even with a solid grasp of Ruby basics and advanced techniques, you're bound to encounter issues. This section provides guidance on troubleshooting common problems, debugging errors, and refining your code.

6.1 Common Syntax Errors

Missing End Keywords

One frequent error for beginners is omitting the end keyword in conditionals, loops, or method definitions. Ruby's error messages will often point to an unexpected end-of-input. Ensure every opening structure (if, while, def, etc.) has a corresponding end.

Before:

```ruby
ruby

def say_hello
  puts "Hello, world!"
# Missing 'end' here
After:
ruby

def say_hello
  puts "Hello, world!"
end
```

6.2 Debugging with Print Statements

A straightforward method for troubleshooting is inserting puts statements to display variable values and program flow. This technique is especially helpful when trying to understand how data changes over time.

Example:

```ruby
ruby

def calculate_total(numbers)
  total = 0
  numbers.each do |num|
    total += num
    puts "Current total: #{total}"  # Debugging
output
  end
  total
end

calculate_total([1, 2, 3, 4, 5])
```

6.3 Using Debugging Tools

Ruby offers debugging tools such as Byebug. To use Byebug, insert require 'byebug' and byebug into your code where you want to pause execution:

```ruby
ruby

require 'byebug'
```

```
def faulty_method
  byebug
  x = 10
  y = 0
  puts x / y
end


# Uncomment the following line to run the faulty
method for debugging.
# faulty_method
```

This allows you to inspect variables and step through your code line by line.

6.4 Handling Runtime Errors

Errors such as division by zero or nil errors are common during development. Implementing error handling with begin-rescue blocks can prevent your program from crashing unexpectedly.

Example:

```
ruby

def safe_divide(a, b)
  begin
    result = a / b
  rescue ZeroDivisionError
    result = "Error: Division by zero is not
allowed."
  end
  result
end

puts safe_divide(10, 0)
```

This approach catches exceptions and allows you to provide a meaningful error message.

6.5 Troubleshooting Data Structure Issues

When working with arrays and hashes, common pitfalls include accessing non-existent keys or indices. Always verify that the data exists before attempting to use it.

Before-and-After Example:

Before (Prone to errors):

```ruby
student = { name: "Alice", grade: "A" }
puts student[:age]  # Returns nil, which might lead
to unexpected behavior.
```

After (Handling missing keys):

```ruby
student = { name: "Alice", grade: "A" }
puts student.fetch(:age, "Age not provided")
```

6.6 Problem-Solving Strategies

Adopt a systematic approach to troubleshooting:

- **Reproduce the Issue:** Isolate the error by running a minimal example.

- **Read Error Messages Carefully:** They often contain hints about what went wrong.

- **Search Documentation and Forums:** The Ruby community is active; many issues have been discussed and resolved online.

- **Refactor Incrementally:** Make small changes and test frequently to pinpoint the source of the problem.

6.7 Final Troubleshooting Tips

- **Stay Organized:** Keep your code well-commented and structured to make it easier to identify errors.

- **Ask for Help:** Utilize community forums like Stack Overflow if you're stuck.

- **Keep Learning:** Each error is an opportunity to deepen your understanding of Ruby.

7. Conclusion & Next Steps

In this chapter, we've covered the fundamentals of Ruby's syntax, control structures, and data structures. You now understand how to work with variables, strings, numbers, and operators; how to control program flow using conditionals and loops; and how to manage data effectively with arrays and hashes.

Summary of Key Points

- **Syntax and Basic Constructs:**
  You learned how to declare variables, work with strings and numbers, and use operators for arithmetic operations. The focus on clear, human-readable syntax makes Ruby approachable for everyone.

- **Control Structures and Flow:**
  Conditional statements and loops are crucial for making decisions and repeating tasks. Exercises and analogies helped clarify how these structures work in everyday scenarios.

- **Data Structures:**
  Arrays and hashes are the foundation for managing collections of data. By understanding how to store, access, and manipulate data, you're better prepared to build more complex programs.

Next Steps

Now that you have a solid grasp of Ruby basics, here are some suggestions to continue your learning journey:

- **Experiment:**
  Modify the example projects in this chapter. Add new features, change conditions, and see how small modifications can alter the behavior of your programs.

- **Deepen Your Understanding:**
  Explore additional resources such as Ruby documentation, online tutorials, and community forums. Engage with other developers to learn best practices and common pitfalls.

- **Build Projects:**
  Start small projects of your own. Whether it's a simple script to automate a task or a more interactive application, applying what you've learned will reinforce your knowledge.

- **Prepare for Advanced Topics:**
  As you get more comfortable, consider learning about Ruby's object-oriented features, exception handling, and eventually frameworks like Ruby on Rails.

Additional Resources

To further your studies, here are some recommended resources:

- **The Official Ruby Documentation:**
  A comprehensive guide to every aspect of Ruby.

- **RubyMonk and Codecademy:**
  Interactive platforms that offer exercises and projects.

- **Books:**
  Titles like *"Programming Ruby"* provide in-depth knowledge and advanced techniques.

- **Community Forums:**
  Engage with communities on Reddit's r/ruby or Stack Overflow to get answers and share ideas.

Final Thoughts

Learning Ruby is a journey, and mastering the basics is the first important step. With the clear syntax, expressive control structures, and versatile data handling features Ruby offers, you're well-equipped to solve a wide range of programming challenges. Remember, every programmer faces challenges, but with persistence and practice, you will become proficient.

This chapter has provided the necessary tools, examples, and exercises to build a strong foundation in Ruby programming. Keep practicing, keep experimenting, and most importantly, enjoy the process of coding. Your next steps could involve tackling more complex projects or exploring advanced Ruby concepts, but the fundamental skills you have acquired here will always be at the heart of your programming endeavors.

Chapter 3: Object-Oriented Programming in Ruby

1. Introduction

Object-oriented programming (OOP) is a programming paradigm that revolves around the concept of "objects" – structures that combine data and behavior. In Ruby, OOP is a central feature, allowing you to organize code in ways that mirror real-world entities. This chapter explores the core principles of object-oriented programming by introducing classes and objects, methods and attributes, and a hands-on exercise where you build your own classes. Whether you're new to programming or an experienced developer looking to strengthen your Ruby skills, mastering OOP is key to building flexible, scalable, and maintainable applications.

In everyday life, think of an object as a tangible item, such as a car. A car has attributes like color, model, and speed; it also has behaviors such as accelerating or braking. Similarly, in Ruby, a class acts as a blueprint for objects. When you define a class, you are specifying the structure and behaviors that any instance of that class will have. For example, a Library class might include attributes such as a list of books and behaviors like checking out a book.

Why Object-Oriented Programming Matters

Organizing your code using classes makes your programs easier to understand, maintain, and extend. When functionality is encapsulated within objects, you can manage complexity by isolating different parts of your program. This modularity allows you to reuse code and collaborate with other developers more effectively. OOP also aligns with many real-world models, meaning that the code you write can closely represent the problem domain you are working with.

Key Terms and Concepts

Before diving in, let's define some essential terminology:

- **Class:** A blueprint for objects. A class defines attributes (data) and methods (behaviors) that its objects will have.

- **Object (Instance):** A concrete example of a class. When you create an object, you allocate memory for that instance and it carries the properties defined in the class.

- **Method:** A function defined inside a class that describes the behaviors of an object. Methods allow objects to perform actions or compute values.

- **Attribute:** A piece of data that represents a property of an object. In Ruby, attributes are typically managed using instance variables.

- **Encapsulation:** The bundling of data and methods into a single unit (class) and restricting access to some of the object's components.

- **Inheritance:** A mechanism where one class can inherit attributes and methods from another class, promoting code reuse.

- **Polymorphism:** The ability for different classes to respond to the same method call in different ways.

By understanding these concepts, you'll be able to write code that is both robust and easy to extend.

Setting the Tone for Exploration

Throughout this chapter, you will find a conversational yet professional style aimed at demystifying the principles of OOP. We'll start with a gentle introduction and build up to more advanced ideas, using everyday examples to illustrate abstract concepts. You are encouraged to pause and experiment with the provided code samples. Modify the examples, add new features, and observe how your changes affect the overall behavior of your program.

The practical exercises included will reinforce your understanding by allowing you to design, build, and test your own Ruby classes. Whether you aim to model a simple library system or develop a contact manager, the skills you acquire here will be applicable to a wide range of programming challenges.

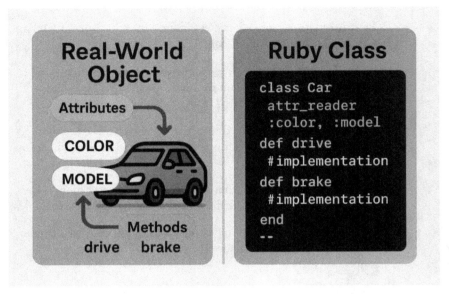

In summary, this chapter serves as your gateway to object-oriented programming in Ruby. You will learn not only the theory behind OOP but also how to apply these ideas practically, making your code more organized and easier to manage. Let's dive into the core concepts and theory behind classes, objects, methods, and attributes.

---

2. Core Concepts and Theory

In this section, we explore the essential ideas behind object-oriented programming in Ruby. The discussion covers how classes and objects form the building blocks of Ruby programs, along with an in-depth look at methods and attributes. Real-life analogies and examples are used throughout to simplify abstract ideas.

2.1 Classes and Objects

What Is a Class?

A class in Ruby is a blueprint that defines the attributes and behaviors common to a particular type of object. When you create a class, you are essentially setting up a template from which multiple instances (objects) can be generated. Consider the concept of a "Book" in a library system. The class might include attributes such as title, author, and publication date, and methods like check_out and return_book.

Here's a simple class definition in Ruby:

```ruby
class Book
  # Constructor method to initialize a new book
  def initialize(title, author)
    @title = title
    @author = author
  end

  # Method to display information about the book
  def display_info
    puts "Title: #{@title}"
    puts "Author: #{author}"
  end
end
```

In the example above, the initialize method sets up new objects with a title and an author. The instance variables (prefixed with @) store these values, and the display_info method prints them.

Everyday Analogy:

Think of a class as a recipe for a cake. The recipe (class) specifies the ingredients (attributes) and steps (methods) required to bake the cake. Each cake (object) you bake from the recipe will have those ingredients and follow the same steps.

Creating Objects

Once a class is defined, you can create objects (instances) from that class using the new keyword:

```ruby
my_book = Book.new("1984", "George Orwell")
my_book.display_info
```

In this case, my_book is an instance of the Book class. It has its own set of attributes that were defined by the class.

Benefits of Using Classes

Using classes provides several benefits:

- **Modularity:** Code is organized into distinct sections, making it easier to manage.

- **Reusability:** Once a class is defined, it can be used to create many objects.

- **Maintainability:** Changes made to the class definition automatically apply to all objects.

- **Real-World Mapping:** Classes allow you to model real-world entities, making your code more intuitive.

2.2 Methods and Attributes

Methods

Methods in Ruby are functions defined within a class that describe the actions an object can perform. They encapsulate behavior and can operate on the object's data. Methods are defined using the def keyword and are followed by the method name and any parameters:

```ruby
class Contact
  def initialize(name, email)
    @name = name
    @email = email
  end

  # Method to display contact information
  def display_contact
    puts "Name: #{@name}"
    puts "Email: #{@email}"
  end
```

```
  # Method to update the email address
  def update_email(new_email)
    @email = new_email
  end
end
```

In the Contact class example above, the display_contact method prints out the contact's details, while the update_email method allows you to change the contact's email address.

Everyday Analogy:
Imagine a smartphone. The phone (object) has various functions (methods) such as calling, texting, or taking a photo. These functions are built into the device (class) and allow the phone to perform actions.

Attributes

Attributes, represented by instance variables, hold the data for each object. In Ruby, instance variables are denoted by an @ symbol and are accessible within the instance methods of a class.

Consider the following example:

ruby

```
class Product
  def initialize(name, price)
    @name = name
    @price = price
  end

  def display_product
    puts "Product: #{@name}, Price: $#{@price}"
  end
end
```

Here, @name and @price are attributes that store the product's information. You can think of them as the properties of an object.

2.3 Encapsulation and Abstraction

Encapsulation is the idea of bundling the data (attributes) and the methods that operate on that data within a single unit – the class. This approach hides the internal state of the object from the outside world and only exposes a well-defined interface.

For example, if you have a BankAccount class, you may want to keep the balance private and only allow it to be modified via deposit and withdrawal methods. This prevents accidental modification of the balance:

```ruby
class BankAccount
  def initialize(owner, balance)
    @owner = owner
    @balance = balance
  end

  def deposit(amount)
    @balance += amount
  end

  def withdraw(amount)
    if amount > @balance
      puts "Insufficient funds"
    else
      @balance -= amount
    end
  end

  def display_balance
    puts "#{@owner}'s balance is: $#{@balance}"
  end
end
```

By encapsulating the balance, you ensure that it can only be changed in controlled ways, which makes your code safer and easier to maintain.

2.4 Inheritance and Polymorphism (Brief Overview)

Inheritance allows one class to inherit properties and methods from another class. This mechanism promotes code reuse. For example, a Vehicle class could define basic attributes and behaviors for all vehicles, and a Car class could inherit from Vehicle while adding its own features.

Polymorphism lets objects of different classes be treated as objects of a common superclass. This means that different classes can define methods with the same name, and Ruby will call the appropriate method depending on the object's actual class.

Although this chapter focuses on basic OOP concepts, understanding inheritance and polymorphism is useful as you progress to more complex topics.

2.5 Summarizing the Theory

To recap, this section covered:

- **Classes and Objects:** How to use classes as blueprints and create instances that encapsulate data and behavior.

- **Methods and Attributes:** How methods perform actions on data stored in instance variables, forming the core of an object's functionality.

- **Encapsulation:** The practice of hiding an object's internal state while exposing a clear interface.

- **Inheritance and Polymorphism:** Briefly touching on how these concepts support code reuse and flexibility.

These fundamental ideas form the backbone of object-oriented programming in Ruby. With this theoretical foundation, you are now prepared to set up the necessary tools and environments for hands-on practice.

3. Tools and Setup

Before you begin coding, it's important to have the right environment. In this section, we detail the tools, platforms, and setup instructions required to develop Ruby applications that utilize object-oriented programming.

3.1 Required Software and Platforms

For developing Ruby OOP applications, you will need the following:

- **Ruby Interpreter:** Ensure you have Ruby installed on your machine. If not, refer to Chapter 1 for installation instructions.

- **Text Editor or Integrated Development Environment (IDE):** Popular choices include Visual Studio Code (VS Code) and

RubyMine. These tools offer syntax highlighting, debugging, and code completion.

- **Terminal or Command Prompt:** This is required for running Ruby scripts and managing your development environment.

- **Version Control System (Optional):** Git can be useful for tracking changes and collaborating on projects.

3.2 Configuring Your Editor

Visual Studio Code (VS Code)

1. **Installation:**
   Download VS Code from the official website and install it following the provided instructions.

2. **Ruby Extensions:**
   Open the Extensions view, search for Ruby-related plugins, and install those that provide syntax highlighting and debugging capabilities.

3. **Settings:**
   Adjust your settings (such as font size and tab spacing) to optimize your coding experience.

RubyMine

1. **Download and Install:**
   RubyMine is a specialized Ruby IDE available from JetBrains. Download it from the official site and follow the installation process.

2. **Project Setup:**
   Configure RubyMine to detect your Ruby installation. This helps with running scripts and debugging.

3.3 Setting Up Your Terminal

Ensure your terminal is ready for Ruby development. On macOS and Linux, the built-in Terminal works well. Windows users can use Command Prompt, PowerShell, or Git Bash. Verify your Ruby installation with the command:

```bash
```

```bash
ruby -v
```
This command should output the Ruby version currently installed.

3.4 Creating a Sample Project Structure

To organize your work, create a new project directory. For instance:

```bash
```

```bash
mkdir ruby_oop_project
cd ruby_oop_project
```
Within this directory, create separate files for your classes and tests as needed. A clean project structure helps maintain clarity and scalability.

3.5 Version Control Setup (Optional)

Using Git is recommended to manage your project's versions:

1. **Initialize a Git Repository:**

```bash
```

```bash
git init
```
2. **Add Files and Make a Commit:**

```bash
```

```bash
git add .
git commit -m "Initial commit: Set up Ruby OOP
project structure"
```
Version control helps you track changes over time and collaborate with others.

3.6 Summary of Tools and Environment Setup

This section covered the essential tools and setup steps required for Ruby development:

- Installation of Ruby and configuration of your text editor or IDE.

- Terminal setup and verification of your Ruby interpreter.

- Organizing your project structure and optionally using Git for version control.

With your development environment ready, you're now prepared to apply object-oriented concepts in practical projects.

---

4. Hands-on Examples & Projects

This extensive section takes you through practical examples and guided projects. Each example demonstrates how to define classes, create objects, work with methods and attributes, and test your code. The examples build on one another to gradually introduce more complex features.

4.1 Example 1: Creating a Simple Class for a Shop

Project: "Product Catalog"

In this example, you will create a Product class that represents items in a shop. This class will have attributes for name, price, and stock quantity, along with methods to display information and update stock.

1. **Create a File:**
   Name it product.rb.

2. **Write the Code:**

```ruby
# product.rb
# A class to represent a product in a shop.

class Product
  # Initialize the product with a name, price, and
stock quantity.
  def initialize(name, price, stock)
    @name = name
    @price = price
    @stock = stock
  end

  # Method to display product information.
  def display
    puts "Product: #{@name}"
    puts "Price: $#{@price}"
```

```
   puts "Stock: #{@stock} units"
  end

  # Method to update stock quantity.
  def update_stock(new_stock)
    @stock = new_stock
    puts "Stock updated to #{@stock} units for
#{@name}."
  end
end

# Create an instance of Product and test its methods.
product = Product.new("Ruby T-Shirt", 19.99, 50)
product.display
product.update_stock(45)
```

3. **Explanation:**

> o   The initialize method sets up the product's attributes.

> o   The display method prints the product details.

> o   The update_stock method allows you to modify the stock.

4. **Run the Script:**
   Execute in the terminal with:

```bash
```

```
ruby product.rb
```

Exercise:
Modify the class to include a discount method that calculates a reduced price.

4.2 Example 2: Building a Basic Contact Manager

Project: "Contact Manager"

This project demonstrates how to define a Contact class with attributes for name, phone number, and email. You will also create methods to display and update contact information.

1. **Create a File:**
   Name it contact_manager.rb.

2. **Write the Code:**

```ruby
# contact_manager.rb
# A simple contact manager using a Contact class.

class Contact
  def initialize(name, phone, email)
    @name = name
    @phone = phone
    @email = email
  end

  # Display contact information.
  def display_contact
    puts "Name: #{@name}"
    puts "Phone: #{@phone}"
    puts "Email: #{@email}"
  end

  # Update contact information.
  def update_contact(new_phone, new_email)
    @phone = new_phone
    @email = new_email
    puts "Contact updated for #{@name}."
  end
end

# Create an instance of Contact.
contact = Contact.new("Jordan", "555-1234",
"jordan@example.com")
contact.display_contact

# Update and display the contact again.
contact.update_contact("555-5678",
"jordan.new@example.com")
contact.display_contact
```

3. **Explanation:**

   o   The initialize method sets up the contact's details.

   o   The display_contact method shows the information.

      o   The update_contact method modifies the contact details.

4. **Run the Script:**
   Execute in the terminal:

```bash
```

```
ruby contact_manager.rb
```
Exercise:
Expand the contact manager to store multiple contacts in an array and include functionality to search by name.

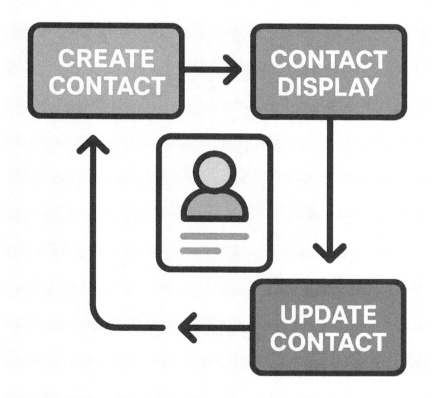

4.3 Example 3: Hands-on Exercise – Create Your Own Class

Project: "Library System"

In this guided project, you will build a mini library system. This exercise reinforces the creation of classes, instance variables, and methods, while encouraging you to add features incrementally.

1. **Create a File:**
   Name it library_system.rb.

2. **Step 1: Define a Book Class**

```ruby
# library_system.rb
# A class representing a book in a library system.

class Book
  attr_accessor :title, :author, :checked_out

  # Initialize the book with title, author, and
checked-out status.
  def initialize(title, author)
    @title = title
    @author = author
    @checked_out = false
  end

  # Display book details.
  def display_info
    status = @checked_out ? "Checked Out" :
"Available"
    puts "Title: #{@title}, Author: #{author},
Status: #{status}"
  end

  # Check out the book.
  def check_out
    if @checked_out
      puts "The book '#{@title}' is already checked
out."
    else
```

```ruby
    @checked_out = true
    puts "You have checked out '#{@title}'."
  end
end

# Return the book.
def return_book
  if @checked_out
    @checked_out = false
    puts "Thank you for returning '#{@title}'."
  else
    puts "The book '#{@title}' was not checked
out."
  end
end
end
```

3. **Step 2: Create a Library Class**

Next, create a class to manage a collection of books.

ruby

```ruby
class Library
  def initialize
    @books = []
  end

  # Add a new book to the library.
  def add_book(book)
    @books << book
    puts "Added '#{book.title}' to the library."
  end

  # Display all books.
  def display_books
    puts "Library Collection:"
    @books.each { |book| book.display_info }
  end

  # Find a book by title.
  def find_book(title)
    @books.find { |book| book.title.downcase ==
title.downcase }
  end
```

```
end
```

4. Step 3: Use the Library System

Finally, combine the classes to simulate a library operation.

```ruby
ruby

# Create a library instance.
library = Library.new

# Create book objects.
book1 = Book.new("1984", "George Orwell")
book2 = Book.new("To Kill a Mockingbird", "Harper
Lee")

# Add books to the library.
library.add_book(book1)
library.add_book(book2)

# Display the library collection.
library.display_books

# Simulate checking out a book.
book = library.find_book("1984")
if book
  book.check_out
end

# Display collection after check out.
library.display_books

# Simulate returning the book.
book.return_book if book

# Display final state of the library.
library.display_books
```

5. Explanation:

- o The Book class uses attr_accessor to automatically create getter and setter methods for its attributes.

- o The Library class maintains an array of books and includes methods to add, display, and search for books.

- o The combined code simulates a realistic scenario where books are added, checked out, and returned.

6. **Run the Script:**
   In the terminal, run:

```bash
```

```
ruby library_system.rb
```
Exercise:
Extend the library system by allowing the removal of books or adding categories to the books.

4.4 Additional Exercises to Practice

As you grow more confident with classes and objects, try the following:

- **Design a Shop System:**
  Create classes for Customer, Product, and Order to simulate an online shop.

- **Build a Simple Game:**
  Create classes such as Player, Enemy, and Game to design a basic text-based adventure.

- **Model a Restaurant:**
  Define classes for MenuItem, Order, and Restaurant to practice handling data and methods together.

Each of these projects reinforces your understanding of object-oriented programming by applying the principles learned in real-world scenarios.

4.5 Recap of Hands-on Examples

This section covered several practical projects:

- A product catalog for a shop.

- A contact manager to handle personal data.

- A comprehensive library system that ties together multiple classes.

- Additional exercises to encourage creative application of OOP principles.

Each project emphasizes clean code practices and includes comments that explain each step, ensuring that you not only learn how to write object-oriented Ruby code but also understand why the code is structured in a particular way.

5. Advanced Techniques & Optimization

After mastering the basics, you might wish to optimize and extend your object-oriented designs. This section explores techniques for writing more efficient and maintainable Ruby code.

5.1 Advanced Class Design

As your projects grow, your classes might become more complex. Consider the following strategies:

- **Separation of Concerns:**
  Divide your code so that each class handles a specific part of the functionality.

- **Modularity:**
  Create mixins or modules to share common behavior across classes.

- **Design Patterns:**
  Study common design patterns (such as Singleton or Observer) to solve recurring design problems.

Example: Using Modules for Shared Behavior

```ruby

# module for formatting output
module Displayable
  def display_header(title)
    puts "=== #{title} ==="
  end
end

class Product
  include Displayable
```

```ruby
def initialize(name, price)
  @name = name
  @price = price
end

def display_info
  display_header("Product Information")
  puts "Name: #{@name}"
  puts "Price: $#{@price}"
end
end
```

This approach keeps your code DRY and improves readability.

5.2 Performance Optimization

For larger applications, optimizing your code can lead to significant improvements:

- **Lazy Evaluation:**
  Use lazy enumerators for large collections to avoid loading unnecessary data.

- **Memoization:**
  Cache expensive method calls to prevent redundant computations.

- **Profiling:**
  Use benchmarking tools to measure and optimize performance-critical sections of your code.

Example: Memoization in a Calculation Method

ruby

```ruby
def factorial(n, memo = {})
  return 1 if n <= 1
  memo[n] ||= n * factorial(n - 1, memo)
end
```

Memoization prevents repeated calculation of the same values, speeding up recursive calls.

5.3 Advanced Error Handling

Robust applications need effective error handling. Instead of letting exceptions crash your program, catch errors and handle them gracefully.

```ruby
class PaymentProcessor
  def process(amount)
    begin
      # Imagine a call to an external payment gateway here
      raise StandardError, "Payment failed" if amount <= 0
      puts "Payment of $#{amount} processed successfully."
    rescue StandardError => e
      puts "Error processing payment: #{e.message}"
    end
  end
end

processor = PaymentProcessor.new
processor.process(-5)
```

5.4 Code Refactoring and Maintenance

As your codebase grows, regularly refactor your code to keep it clean and maintainable. This involves:

- **Extracting Methods:**
  Break long methods into smaller, reusable methods.

- **Renaming Variables:**
  Use descriptive names that make the code self-documenting.

- **Removing Duplication:**
  Consolidate duplicate code into shared methods or modules.

5.5 Best Practices for Advanced Ruby OOP

- **Write Unit Tests:**
  Use frameworks like RSpec to ensure your classes behave as expected.

- **Use Documentation:**
  Comment your code and maintain documentation to help future you or your teammates understand your design decisions.

- **Follow Community Guidelines:**
  Adhere to style guides (such as the Ruby Style Guide) to produce consistent, readable code.

5.6 Recap of Advanced Techniques

This section discussed several advanced topics:

- Modular design using mixins.

- Performance improvements through lazy evaluation and memoization.

- Robust error handling to prevent crashes.

- Refactoring practices that lead to clean, maintainable code.

By integrating these techniques into your development process, you can write Ruby code that is not only functional but also efficient and scalable.

---

6. Troubleshooting and Problem-Solving

Even well-designed code can encounter issues. In this section, we explore common challenges in object-oriented programming and provide strategies for resolving them.

6.1 Common OOP Issues

Undefined Methods or Variables

One frequent issue is attempting to call a method or access a variable that hasn't been defined. Ruby's error messages will often indicate that a method is "undefined." Always verify that your class definitions include the methods you intend to call and that instance variables are properly initialized.

Incorrect Use of self

Using self incorrectly can lead to unexpected behavior. Remember that self refers to the current object, and using it appropriately is crucial in method definitions and attribute access.

6.2 Debugging Techniques

Print Debugging

Insert puts statements in your methods to trace the flow of execution and inspect variable values:

```ruby
def update_stock(new_stock)
  puts "Updating stock from #{@stock} to
#{new_stock}"
  @stock = new_stock
end
```

Using Byebug

For a more in-depth approach, use the Byebug gem to step through your code:

```ruby
require 'byebug'

def faulty_method
  byebug
  # Code that might be causing issues
end
```

This allows you to inspect the state of your program and better understand where errors occur.

6.3 Handling Exceptions

Wrap sections of your code in begin-rescue blocks to catch exceptions and provide meaningful error messages. This is especially useful in production systems where a crash is not acceptable.

```ruby
def process_payment(amount)
```

```ruby
  begin
    raise "Invalid amount" if amount <= 0
    # Simulate payment processing
    puts "Processing payment of $#{amount}"
  rescue => e
    puts "Error: #{e.message}"
  end
end
```

6.4 Before-and-After Code Examples

Here's an example of code before refactoring and after applying error handling and debugging improvements.

Before:

ruby

```ruby
def checkout(book)
  # Assume book is a Book object
  if book.checked_out
    puts "Book is already checked out."
  else
    book.checked_out = true
    puts "Checked out #{book.title}"
  end
end
```

After:

ruby

```ruby
def checkout(book)
  begin
    if book.checked_out
      puts "Book '#{book.title}' is already checked
out."
    else
      book.checked_out = true
      puts "Successfully checked out
'#{book.title}'."
    end
  rescue NoMethodError => e
    puts "Error: #{e.message}. Please verify that the
book object is valid."
  end
```

```
end
```

6.5 Strategies for Effective Problem-Solving

- **Isolate the Issue:**
  Reduce your code to the smallest example that reproduces the error.

- **Consult Documentation:**
  Use Ruby's extensive documentation and community forums for guidance.

- **Collaborate:**
  Pair programming or seeking feedback from peers can uncover issues you might have overlooked.

6.6 Recap of Troubleshooting Techniques

This section provided methods to identify, debug, and resolve common problems in Ruby's OOP:

- Printing debug information.

- Using Byebug for step-by-step analysis.

- Implementing error handling for unexpected situations.

By adopting these practices, you'll become more confident in diagnosing and fixing issues in your object-oriented Ruby code.

---

7. Conclusion & Next Steps

As we conclude this chapter on object-oriented programming in Ruby, let's review what we've covered and look ahead to further learning opportunities.

Summary of Main Points

- **Classes and Objects:**
  You learned how to define classes and create objects that encapsulate both data and behavior. Through real-world analogies such as a library or shop, you saw how classes model tangible entities.

- **Methods and Attributes:**
  The chapter demonstrated how methods enable objects to perform actions, while attributes store their state. The examples, such as the contact manager and product catalog, illustrated these concepts in practical applications.

- **Hands-on Exercise:**
  The library system project provided a guided exercise in designing, testing, and extending your own classes. This practical approach reinforces the theoretical ideas discussed.

- **Advanced Techniques:**
  We discussed strategies for optimizing class design, improving performance, and refactoring code to maintain clarity and efficiency.

- **Troubleshooting:**
  Common pitfalls and debugging strategies were presented to help you resolve issues that arise during development.

Next Steps for Continued Learning

Now that you have a solid foundation in object-oriented programming with Ruby, consider the following:

- **Experiment with Your Own Projects:**
  Build new applications that incorporate classes, inheritance, and modules. Try creating a small game or a simulation of a real-world system.

- **Explore Inheritance and Polymorphism:**
  In future chapters, delve deeper into advanced OOP concepts such as inheritance, polymorphism, and design patterns.

- **Study Ruby Libraries:**
  Look into popular Ruby libraries and frameworks (for example, Ruby on Rails) to see how OOP principles are applied in large-scale applications.

- **Engage with the Community:**
  Join Ruby forums, attend meetups, and participate in online discussions to learn best practices and get feedback on your projects.

Final Thoughts

Object-oriented programming is a powerful way to structure your code, making it more organized, reusable, and easier to understand. By mastering classes, objects, methods, and attributes, you now have the tools to create programs that model real-world scenarios. Each project and exercise in this chapter has been designed to build your confidence and provide practical insights that you can apply immediately.

Keep experimenting with new ideas and don't be afraid to refactor your code as you learn. The principles of encapsulation, modularity, and clean design are not just academic concepts—they are the foundation of robust, maintainable software. As you continue to explore Ruby and other programming languages, these object-oriented techniques will serve you well in solving complex problems and developing sophisticated applications.

Remember, programming is a continuous learning process. Every error you encounter and every solution you devise contributes to your growth as a developer. Take the time to reflect on the projects in this chapter, and consider how you can extend them further or apply similar principles to new challenges.

Thank you for taking the time to work through this chapter on object-oriented programming in Ruby. With this solid grounding in OOP, you are ready to tackle more advanced topics and build applications that truly mirror the complexities of the real world.

Happy coding, and best of luck on your continued journey in mastery Ruby!

Chapter 4: Building Web Applications

1. Introduction

Web applications have become the backbone of modern software, powering everything from simple personal blogs to complex enterprise systems. In this chapter, we explore how to build web applications using Ruby. You will learn about popular frameworks, including Ruby on Rails and Sinatra, and gain step-by-step guidance for creating a basic web app. Additionally, we will cover database integration and guide you through a complete project: a Task Manager Application.

At its core, a web application is a program that runs on a server and delivers dynamic content to users through a web browser. Building these applications involves several layers, including routing requests to the correct controllers, rendering views, and interacting with databases to persist data. In Ruby, the choice of framework significantly influences how these tasks are managed. Ruby on Rails, for example, is a full-stack framework that provides conventions over configuration and a rich ecosystem, while Sinatra offers a lightweight, flexible alternative for smaller projects.

Why Should You Care?

Whether you're a beginner eager to create your first dynamic website, a professional looking to expand your toolkit, or a hobbyist exploring new challenges, learning to build web applications in Ruby opens up a world of possibilities. With clear, concise syntax and a friendly developer community, Ruby is an excellent choice for web development. This chapter not only explains the fundamental concepts behind web apps but also demonstrates how to implement these ideas through practical examples.

Key Concepts and Terminology

Before diving deeper, it's important to understand some key terms:

- **Framework:** A collection of libraries and tools that provide a structured way to build web applications. In Ruby, Rails and Sinatra are two common examples.

- **Routing:** The process of directing incoming HTTP requests to the appropriate code that handles them.

- **Controller:** A component that processes requests, interacts with models, and renders views.

- **View:** The user interface, typically rendered as HTML, which presents data to the user.

- **Model:** Represents the data layer and business logic. Models handle data validation, storage, and retrieval.

- **ORM (Object-Relational Mapping):** A technique that allows you to interact with a database using Ruby objects rather than writing SQL directly.

- **CRUD:** An acronym for Create, Read, Update, and Delete—the four basic operations for managing data.

Setting the Tone

This chapter is designed to be engaging and practical. Each section provides clear explanations alongside code examples that illustrate key points. You'll see how web frameworks abstract many complexities, letting you focus on solving real-world problems. Our aim is to make complex topics accessible, so expect analogies (like comparing a controller to a traffic director) and step-by-step guides that walk you through code implementation.

By the end of this chapter, you'll have a clear understanding of how to choose a web framework that suits your needs, set up your development environment, build a basic web application, integrate with a database, and ultimately, develop a complete task manager application. These skills are directly applicable to many real-world projects and will serve as a foundation for further exploration into web development.

Let's now begin our journey into building web applications with Ruby.

2. Core Concepts and Theory

In this section, we delve into the fundamental concepts underlying web development with Ruby. We'll discuss how to choose the right framework, explore the architecture of a web application, and explain how routing, controllers, views, and models work together. Real-world examples and analogies are used to simplify these concepts.

2.1 Choosing a Framework

Ruby offers a choice of frameworks to suit different project needs. Two popular options are Ruby on Rails and Sinatra.

Ruby on Rails

Ruby on Rails (often just "Rails") is a full-stack framework that follows the "convention over configuration" philosophy. This means Rails makes many decisions for you, providing sensible defaults that accelerate development. With built-in support for ORM (via ActiveRecord), templating, routing, and testing, Rails is ideal for large-scale applications that require a robust structure.

Strengths of Rails:

- **Rapid Development:** Pre-configured structure speeds up the development process.

- **Rich Ecosystem:** Numerous plugins (gems) and a large community.

- **Convention over Configuration:** Reduces boilerplate code.

Sinatra

Sinatra is a micro-framework that offers a lightweight alternative to Rails. It provides the basic tools needed to handle HTTP requests and responses but leaves many decisions up to the developer. Sinatra is well-suited for small projects, APIs, or when you need more flexibility and minimal overhead.

Strengths of Sinatra:

- **Simplicity:** Minimalist and easy to understand.

- **Flexibility:** Fewer conventions allow for custom implementations.

- **Lightweight:** Ideal for small applications and microservices.

Real-World Analogy:
Imagine Rails as a fully-furnished apartment where everything is already in place for you, whereas Sinatra is like renting a bare-bones studio where you set up your own furniture. Your choice depends on whether you need the full package or prefer to build things from scratch.

2.2 The Anatomy of a Web Application

A typical web application comprises several layers:

- **Routing:** Maps URLs to specific code (controllers).

- **Controllers:** Process incoming requests, perform business logic, and determine the response.

- **Views:** Render the final output, often as HTML.

- **Models:** Represent the data and interact with the database.

Routing

Routing is the process that takes an incoming URL and directs it to the correct controller action. For example, in Rails, routes are defined in a file (usually config/routes.rb) and look something like this:

```ruby
Rails.application.routes.draw do
  get 'tasks', to: 'tasks#index'
  post 'tasks', to: 'tasks#create'
  # Additional routes...
end
In Sinatra, routing is even simpler:
ruby

require 'sinatra'
```

```
get '/tasks' do
  # Code to display tasks
end

post '/tasks' do
  # Code to create a task
end
```

Analogy:

Routing is like a postal system where each address (URL) is matched with a specific delivery route (controller action).

Controllers

Controllers serve as the intermediary between the user's request and the application's logic. They fetch data from models and pass it to views. In Rails, a controller might look like this:

```ruby
class TasksController < ApplicationController
  def index
    @tasks = Task.all
  end

  def create
    @task = Task.new(task_params)
    if @task.save
      redirect_to tasks_path
    else
      render :new
    end
  end

  private

  def task_params
    params.require(:task).permit(:title,
:description)
  end
end
```

Explanation:

The index action retrieves all tasks, while the create action handles task creation. The private task_params method secures the data coming from the user.

Views

Views are the presentation layer of your application. They typically contain HTML and embedded Ruby (ERB) code to dynamically render content. A simple ERB view might look like this:

erb

```
<!-- app/views/tasks/index.html.erb -->
<h1>Task List</h1>
<ul>
  <% @tasks.each do |task| %>
    <li><%= task.title %>: <%= task.description
%></li>
  <% end %>
</ul>
```

Analogy:
Think of views as the storefront of a shop. They display the products (data) in an attractive manner to the user.

Models

Models represent the data layer and are responsible for data validation and business logic. In Rails, models typically inherit from ActiveRecord::Base:

ruby

```
class Task < ApplicationRecord
  validates :title, presence: true
  validates :description, presence: true
end
```

Explanation:
Here, the Task model ensures that every task has a title and a description before saving it to the database.

2.3 Integrating Databases

Databases are crucial to storing persistent data. Ruby frameworks like Rails use Object-Relational Mapping (ORM) to abstract database interactions. ActiveRecord in Rails allows you to work with database records as Ruby objects.

CRUD Operations

CRUD stands for Create, Read, Update, and Delete—the basic operations you perform on data:

- **Create:** Adding new records.

- **Read:** Retrieving data.

- **Update:** Modifying existing records.

- **Delete:** Removing records.

Example using ActiveRecord:

```ruby
# Creating a new task
task = Task.new(title: "Buy groceries", description:
"Milk, Bread, Eggs")
task.save

# Reading tasks
tasks = Task.all

# Updating a task
task.update(title: "Buy groceries and fruits")

# Deleting a task
task.destroy
```

Real-World Analogy:
Imagine a library catalog where books can be added, viewed, updated, or removed. The ORM acts as a translator between Ruby objects and database records.

2.4 Framework Comparison: Rails vs. Sinatra

Let's summarize the strengths and differences:

- **Ruby on Rails:**

  o Full-featured with built-in ORM, routing, and scaffolding.

  o Ideal for complex, data-driven applications.

  o Steeper learning curve due to conventions.

- Sinatra:

  o Minimalistic and flexible.

  o Best for small applications, APIs, or microservices.

  o Less "magic" and more manual configuration.

Choosing between these frameworks depends on your project's size, complexity, and personal preference. Rails may accelerate development for larger projects, while Sinatra provides simplicity and control for smaller ones.

RUBY ON RAILS VS. SINATRA

RUBY ON RAILS	SINATRA
Full-stack framework	Lightweight framework
MVC	No enforced architecture
Convention over configuration	Explicit configuration
Many built-in libraries	Minimal built-in libraries
Large community	Smaller community

2.5 Summarizing the Theory

To summarize:

- **Choosing a Framework:** Understand your project requirements to select Rails or Sinatra.

- **Application Architecture:** Recognize how routing, controllers, views, and models interact.

- **Database Integration:** Learn the basics of CRUD operations and ORM.

- **Real-World Examples:** Use analogies to relate web application components to everyday systems.

With these core concepts in mind, you are ready to set up the necessary tools and start building your web application.

---

3. Tools and Setup

A smooth development experience starts with the right tools. In this section, we outline the software and configurations needed to build web applications with Ruby.

3.1 Required Software and Platforms

For web development with Ruby, ensure you have the following:

- **Ruby Interpreter:** Verify Ruby is installed (see Chapter 1 for installation details).

- **Web Framework:** Choose Rails or Sinatra based on your project needs.

- **Database:** For Rails, SQLite is often the default, but you may also use PostgreSQL or MySQL.

- **Text Editor or IDE:** Visual Studio Code, RubyMine, or any editor that supports Ruby.

- **Version Control:** Git is recommended to manage your project files and collaborate with others.

3.2 Installing a Framework

Ruby on Rails Installation

1. **Install Rails Gem:**
   Open your terminal and run:

bash

```
gem install rails
```

2. **Create a New Rails Application:**
   For example, to create a task manager app:

bash

```
rails new task_manager_app
cd task_manager_app
```

3. **Run the Rails Server:**
   Start the server with:

bash

```
rails server
```

Open your browser and navigate to http://localhost:3000 to see your app in action.

Sinatra Installation

1. **Install Sinatra Gem:**
   In your terminal, run:

bash

```
gem install sinatra
```

2. **Create a New File:**
   For example, create a file called app.rb with basic Sinatra code:

ruby

```
require 'sinatra'

get '/' do
  "Hello from Sinatra!"
end
```

3. **Run the Sinatra App:**
   Execute:

```bash
ruby app.rb
Open http://localhost:4567 in your browser to see the output.
```

3.3 Database Setup

Using SQLite with Rails

Rails comes with SQLite as the default database. To set it up:

- Check the config/database.yml file for configuration.

- Run migrations with:

```bash
rails db:migrate
```

Using ActiveRecord with Sinatra

If using Sinatra, you can integrate ActiveRecord by adding it to your Gemfile and configuring a database connection. For example:

```ruby
# Gemfile
gem 'activerecord'
gem 'sinatra-activerecord'
gem 'sqlite3'
Then run:
bash

bundle install
Configure the database in a file such as
config/database.yml and connect in your app.rb.
```

3.4 Configuring Your Editor

For a streamlined workflow:

- **Visual Studio Code:**
  Install Ruby extensions and configure your workspace with tasks for running tests and servers.

- **RubyMine:**
  Use built-in project templates and debugging tools for Rails projects.

3.5 Project Structure and Version Control

Organize your project files logically. For Rails, the default structure is well-organized into folders like app, config, db, etc. For Sinatra, you may create directories for routes, views, and models.

```
Initialize Git:
bash

git init
git add .
git commit -m "Initial commit: Setup web application
project"
```

3.6 Summary of Tools and Setup

To recap:

- Install Ruby and your chosen web framework.

- Configure a database (SQLite, PostgreSQL, etc.).

- Set up your editor with necessary plugins.

- Organize your project and use version control.

With your environment ready, it's time to start coding your web application.

---

4. Hands-on Examples & Projects

This section provides a detailed walkthrough of building a web application from scratch. We will start with simple examples to demonstrate routing, controllers, views, and models, and then move on to a complete project: a Task Manager Application.

4.1 Example 1: Creating a Basic Web App with Rails

Step 1: Generate a New Rails Application

In your terminal, run:

```bash
```

```
rails new task_manager_app
cd task_manager_app
```
Rails creates a new project with a predefined structure that separates concerns into folders (models, views, controllers).

Step 2: Understanding the Structure

- **config/routes.rb:**
  Define the routes that map URLs to controller actions.

- **app/controllers:**
  Contains controller files that manage HTTP requests.

- **app/views:**
  Holds view templates (ERB files) that render HTML.

- **app/models:**
  Contains model files that interact with the database.

Step 3: Creating a Controller and Route

Generate a controller for tasks:

```bash
```

```
rails generate controller Tasks index new create
This command creates a TasksController with actions
and corresponding view files.
Edit config/routes.rb:
ruby
```

```ruby
Rails.application.routes.draw do
  root "tasks#index"
  resources :tasks, only: [:index, :new, :create]
end
```

This sets the home page to the tasks index and creates RESTful routes for tasks.

Step 4: Building the Controller

In app/controllers/tasks_controller.rb, modify the code:

ruby

```ruby
class TasksController < ApplicationController
  def index
    @tasks = Task.all
  end

  def new
    @task = Task.new
  end

  def create
    @task = Task.new(task_params)
    if @task.save
      redirect_to tasks_path, notice: "Task created successfully."
    else
      render :new
    end
  end

  private

  def task_params
    params.require(:task).permit(:title, :description)
  end
end
```

This controller handles listing tasks, rendering a form for new tasks, and saving tasks.

Step 5: Creating Views

Create a view for the index action in app/views/tasks/index.html.erb:

erb

```erb
<h1>Task List</h1>
<%= link_to "New Task", new_task_path %>
<ul>
```

```erb
<% @tasks.each do |task| %>
  <li>
    <strong><%= task.title %></strong>: <%=
task.description %>
  </li>
<% end %>
</ul>
```

And a form for new tasks in
app/views/tasks/new.html.erb:

erb

```erb
<h1>New Task</h1>
<%= form_with model: @task, local: true do |form| %>
  <p>
    <%= form.label :title %><br>
    <%= form.text_field :title %>
  </p>
  <p>
    <%= form.label :description %><br>
    <%= form.text_area :description %>
  </p>
  <p>
    <%= form.submit "Create Task" %>
  </p>
<% end %>
<%= link_to "Back", tasks_path %>
```

Step 6: Creating the Model and Database Migration

Generate a model:

bash

```bash
rails generate model Task title:string
description:text
```

Run the migration:

bash

```bash
rails db:migrate
```

Step 7: Running the Application

Start the Rails server:

```bash
bash

rails server
Visit http://localhost:3000 to see the basic web
application in action.
```

4.2 Example 2: Creating a Basic Web App with Sinatra

For a more lightweight approach, we can build a similar application using Sinatra.

Step 1: Setup

Create a new directory:

```bash
bash

mkdir sinatra_task_manager
cd sinatra_task_manager
Create a file called app.rb with the following code:
ruby

require 'sinatra'
require 'sinatra/activerecord'
require './models/task'

set :database, {adapter: "sqlite3", database:
"db/tasks.sqlite3"}

get '/' do
  @tasks = Task.all
  erb :index
end

get '/tasks/new' do
  erb :new
end

post '/tasks' do
  task = Task.new(title: params[:title], description:
params[:description])
  if task.save
    redirect '/'
```

```
else
    erb :new
  end
end
```

Step 2: Create the Model

Create a folder called models and inside it a file task.rb:

```ruby

class Task < ActiveRecord::Base
  validates :title, presence: true
end
```

Step 3: Create Views

Create a folder called views with two files: index.erb and new.erb.

index.erb:

```erb

<!DOCTYPE html>
<html>
  <head>
    <title>Task Manager</title>
  </head>
  <body>
    <h1>Task List</h1>
    <a href="/tasks/new">New Task</a>
    <ul>
      <% @tasks.each do |task| %>
        <li><strong><%= task.title %></strong>: <%=
task.description %></li>
      <% end %>
    </ul>
  </body>
</html>
```

new.erb:
```erb

<!DOCTYPE html>
<html>
  <head>
    <title>New Task</title>
  </head>
```

```html
<body>
  <h1>New Task</h1>
  <form action="/tasks" method="post">
    <p>
      <label for="title">Title</label><br>
      <input type="text" name="title" id="title">
    </p>
    <p>
      <label
for="description">Description</label><br>
      <textarea name="description"
id="description"></textarea>
    </p>
    <p>
      <input type="submit" value="Create Task">
    </p>
  </form>
  <a href="/">Back</a>
</body>
</html>
```

Step 4: Database Migration

Create a migration file to build the tasks table. You can use ActiveRecord's migration by creating a file db/migrate/001_create_tasks.rb:

```ruby
class CreateTasks < ActiveRecord::Migration[6.0]
  def change
    create_table :tasks do |t|
      t.string :title
      t.text :description
      t.timestamps
    end
  end
end
```

```
Then run:
```

```bash
rake db:migrate
```

Step 5: Running the Sinatra App

Start your Sinatra application:

```bash
```

```
ruby app.rb
Visit http://localhost:4567 to see your web app.
```

4.3 Project: Task Manager Application

Now, let's build a complete Task Manager Application using Ruby on Rails. This project integrates routing, controllers, views, models, and database operations into one cohesive application.

Step 1: Project Setup

Create a new Rails project if you haven't already:

```bash
```

```
rails new task_manager_app
cd task_manager_app
```

Step 2: Generate Scaffold for Tasks

Use Rails scaffolding to generate a basic CRUD interface:

bash

```
rails generate scaffold Task title:string
description:text status:string
```
This command creates a model, views, controller, and migration file for tasks.

Step 3: Migrate the Database

Run the migration:

bash

```
rails db:migrate
```
Step 4: Review and Customize the Code

Examine the generated files in app/controllers/tasks_controller.rb and app/views/tasks. Customize as needed; for example, add a default value for status in the model:

ruby

```
class Task < ApplicationRecord
  validates :title, presence: true
  before_create :set_default_status

  private

  def set_default_status
    self.status ||= "pending"
  end
end
```

Step 5: Enhance the Views

Modify the index view (app/views/tasks/index.html.erb) to include links for editing, deleting, and viewing tasks:

erb

```
<h1>Task Manager</h1>
```

```erb
<%= link_to "New Task", new_task_path, class: "btn
btn-primary" %>
<table>
  <thead>
    <tr>
      <th>Title</th>
      <th>Description</th>
      <th>Status</th>
      <th>Actions</th>
    </tr>
  </thead>
  <tbody>
    <% @tasks.each do |task| %>
      <tr>
        <td><%= task.title %></td>
        <td><%= task.description %></td>
        <td><%= task.status %></td>
        <td>
          <%= link_to "Show", task_path(task) %>
          <%= link_to "Edit", edit_task_path(task) %>
          <%= link_to "Delete", task_path(task),
method: :delete, data: { confirm: "Are you sure?" }
%>
        </td>
      </tr>
    <% end %>
  </tbody>
</table>
```

Step 6: Styling and User Experience

Add basic CSS to improve the user interface (for example, in app/assets/stylesheets/application.css):

css

```css
table {
  width: 100%;
  border-collapse: collapse;
  margin-top: 20px;
}

th, td {
  border: 1px solid #ddd;
  padding: 8px;
```

```
}

th {
  background-color: #f2f2f2;
}
```

Step 7: Testing the Application

Run the Rails server:

```
bash
```

```
rails server
Navigate to http://localhost:3000 and test adding,
updating, and deleting tasks.
```

Step 8: Adding Extra Features

Once the basic task manager is working, consider adding features such as:

- **Filtering by Status:**
  Allow users to filter tasks based on their status.

- **Task Due Dates:**
  Add a date field and display upcoming deadlines.

- **User Authentication:**
  Integrate a simple user login system to manage tasks per user.

4.4 Recap of Hands-on Projects

In this section, you built:

- A basic web app with Rails.

- A similar application using Sinatra.

- A full-featured Task Manager Application with CRUD operations.

Each project demonstrates the integration of routing, controllers, views, models, and database operations. The hands-on examples reinforce theoretical concepts and illustrate how to apply these ideas to solve real-world problems.

5. Advanced Techniques & Optimization

With a basic Task Manager Application in place, you can now explore advanced techniques to improve performance, scalability, and maintainability.

5.1 Advanced Routing and RESTful Design

As your application grows, designing clean, RESTful routes becomes essential. Follow these best practices:

- Use resourceful routing to simplify URL patterns.

- Group similar routes under namespaces.

- Leverage Rails' routing helpers to reduce hard-coded URLs.

Example: Nested Routes

For instance, if you add a feature to manage comments on tasks:

```ruby

resources :tasks do
  resources :comments, only: [:create, :destroy]
end
```
This organizes your routes logically and keeps your code clean.

5.2 Caching and Performance Optimization

Optimize your Rails application by:

- **Caching Views:**
  Use fragment caching to reduce rendering times.

- **Query Optimization:**
  Use eager loading (with .includes) to minimize database queries.

- **Asset Pipeline:**
  Compress and combine CSS and JavaScript files for faster load times.

Example: Eager Loading

ruby

```
@tasks = Task.includes(:comments).all
```
This minimizes the number of database queries when displaying tasks with comments.

5.3 Advanced Database Techniques

For more robust applications:

- **Indexing:**
  Add indexes to frequently searched columns.

- **Migrations:**
  Keep your database schema up to date with incremental migrations.

- **Data Validation and Callbacks:**
  Use model validations and callbacks to enforce business rules.

Example: Adding an Index

In a migration file:

ruby

```
add_index :tasks, :status
```

5.4 Integrating Third-Party APIs

Extend your application's functionality by integrating external APIs. For example, you might use an API to send email notifications when a task is updated.

Example: Using the HTTParty Gem

ruby

```
require 'httparty'

response =
HTTParty.get("https://api.example.com/notify", query:
{ task_id: task.id })
puts response.body
```

5.5 Advanced Frontend Integration

While Rails handles the backend, consider integrating modern frontend frameworks (like React or Vue.js) to improve user experience. Rails' API mode and Sinatra's flexibility make them suitable backends for single-page applications (SPAs).

5.6 Code Refactoring and Best Practices

As your codebase grows, refactoring is key:

- **Modularization:**
  Break controllers and models into smaller, reusable components.

- **Testing:**
  Write unit tests with RSpec to catch issues early.

- **Documentation:**
  Maintain clear documentation and inline comments to help future developers.

5.7 Summary of Advanced Techniques

By applying these techniques, you can transform your basic Task Manager Application into a high-performance, scalable system. The focus should be on:

- Clean, maintainable code.

- Optimized database queries.

- Effective use of caching.

- Robust error handling and logging.

6. Troubleshooting and Problem-Solving

Even the best-designed web applications encounter challenges. This section offers strategies for identifying, diagnosing, and resolving common issues.

6.1 Common Issues in Web Application Development

Routing Errors

- **Symptoms:**
  "No route matches..." errors.

- **Solution:**
  Verify your routes.rb file. Use rails routes to display all defined routes and ensure they match your controller actions.

Database Connection Problems

- **Symptoms:**
  Errors connecting to the database or migrating.

- **Solution:**
  Check your database.yml file for correct settings. Ensure that the database service is running and that you've run the necessary migrations.

View Rendering Issues

- **Symptoms:**
  Blank pages or errors in views.

- **Solution:**
  Ensure your view files are named correctly and that instance variables (like @tasks) are properly set in the controller.

6.2 Debugging Techniques

Log Analysis

Review Rails logs (found in log/development.log) to trace errors and identify problematic code sections.

Interactive Debugging

Use tools such as Byebug:

```ruby
require 'byebug'
```

byebug
This pauses execution, allowing you to inspect variables and flow.

Print Statements

Add temporary puts statements in controllers or models to understand data flow.

6.3 Error Handling and Recovery

Implement error handling in your controllers and models. For example, wrap database calls in begin-rescue blocks to gracefully handle exceptions:

ruby

```ruby
begin
  @task = Task.find(params[:id])
rescue ActiveRecord::RecordNotFound => e
  flash[:error] = "Task not found"
  redirect_to tasks_path
end
```

6.4 Before-and-After Examples

Consider a scenario where a task creation fails due to missing parameters. Instead of allowing the application to crash, you can improve the code:
Before:

ruby

```ruby
def create
  @task = Task.new(task_params)
  if @task.save
    redirect_to tasks_path
  else
    render :new
  end
end
```

After (with better error messaging):

ruby

```ruby
def create
  @task = Task.new(task_params)
  if @task.save
```

```
    redirect_to tasks_path, notice: "Task created
successfully."
  else
    flash.now[:error] =
@task.errors.full_messages.join(", ")
    render :new
  end
end
```

6.5 Troubleshooting Tools

- **Rails Console:**
  Use rails console to experiment with models and test code snippets.

- **Browser Developer Tools:**
  Inspect HTTP requests, view source, and monitor JavaScript errors.

- **Third-Party Services:**
  Utilize error monitoring tools like Sentry or Rollbar to track issues in production.

6.6 Summary of Troubleshooting Techniques

Effective troubleshooting involves:

- Systematic isolation of the error.

- Use of debugging tools and logging.

- Implementing robust error handling in your code.

- Continuous testing and validation.

By following these strategies, you can resolve issues quickly and improve the stability of your web application.

7. Conclusion & Next Steps

In this chapter, we covered the full spectrum of building web applications with Ruby—from choosing the right framework to constructing a complete

Task Manager Application. Let's summarize the key points and discuss how you can continue to grow your skills.

7.1 Summary of Key Points

- **Choosing a Framework:**
  We compared Ruby on Rails and Sinatra, discussing their strengths and ideal use cases.

- **Building a Basic Web App:**
  We walked through setting up routing, controllers, views, and models, first with Rails, then with Sinatra.

- **Database Integration:**
  You learned how to perform CRUD operations using an ORM, integrating a database into your application.

- **Task Manager Project:**
  A full-featured web application was built step-by-step, illustrating the entire process from model creation to view rendering.

- **Advanced Techniques:**
  Topics such as performance optimization, advanced routing, caching, and code refactoring were introduced.

- **Troubleshooting:**
  Common issues were discussed along with practical strategies for debugging and error recovery.

7.2 Next Steps for Continued Learning

Now that you have a solid foundation in building web applications with Ruby, here are some suggestions for moving forward:

- **Experiment Further:**
  Enhance the Task Manager Application by adding features like user authentication, real-time notifications, or integration with external APIs.

- **Explore Advanced Frameworks:**
  Deepen your understanding of Rails by exploring topics such as Action Cable (for real-time features), background job processing, and API mode.

- **Learn Frontend Integration:**
  Consider learning a modern frontend framework (React, Vue.js, or Angular) to build more interactive user interfaces while using Rails as an API backend.

- **Contribute to Open Source:**
  Get involved in the Ruby community by contributing to open-source projects or joining local meetups and online forums.

7.3 Additional Resources

To further your journey, consider the following resources:

- **Official Documentation:**
  The Ruby on Rails Guides and Sinatra documentation provide in-depth explanations and best practices.

- **Books:**
  "Agile Web Development with Rails" and "Sinatra Up and Running" are excellent starting points.

- **Online Courses:**
  Platforms like Codecademy, Udemy, and Coursera offer courses on Ruby web development.

- **Community Forums:**
  Engage with communities on Stack Overflow, Reddit's r/rails, or the Ruby on Rails Link community for support and inspiration.

7.4 Final Thoughts

Building web applications is both a creative and technical pursuit. With the concepts and projects covered in this chapter, you now have the tools to transform your ideas into functional, dynamic web apps. Remember that every project is a learning experience—refactor your code, experiment with new features, and don't be afraid to tackle challenges.

The skills you have gained here lay the groundwork for more advanced topics in web development. Continue practicing, learning, and collaborating with others in the community. The journey to becoming a proficient web developer is ongoing, and each new project will help you hone your craft.

Thank you for working through this chapter on building web applications with Ruby. With a clear understanding of frameworks, routing, controllers, views, models, and database integration, you are well-prepared to create sophisticated web applications that address real-world needs.

Happy coding, and best of luck on your journey into the world of Ruby web development!

Chapter 5: Advanced Ruby Concepts

1. Introduction

Ruby has long been celebrated for its simplicity and expressiveness. As you progress from mastering the basics to more complex applications, it becomes essential to deepen your understanding of advanced Ruby concepts. This chapter focuses on three critical areas that will help you become a more proficient Ruby developer: error handling and debugging, the use of modules, mixins, and libraries to organize and reuse code, and testing your code using popular testing frameworks.

The Significance of Advanced Concepts

Why should you care about these topics? In real-world projects, bugs and unexpected behavior are inevitable. Robust error handling and effective debugging strategies save you time and frustration by making it easier to pinpoint issues. Equally important is the ability to organize your code into modular, reusable components. Ruby's flexible system of modules and mixins not only helps reduce repetition but also makes it simpler to maintain and scale your projects. Finally, writing tests for your code ensures that as your application grows, new changes don't break existing functionality. In short, mastering these advanced topics will make your code more reliable, maintainable, and professional.

Key Concepts and Terminology

Before diving into the specifics, let's define some important terms:

- **Error Handling:** Techniques for intercepting and managing errors during program execution to prevent crashes.

- **Debugging:** The process of identifying, isolating, and fixing bugs in your code.

- **Module:** A collection of methods and constants that can be mixed into classes to share functionality.

- **Mixin:** A way to include the functionality of a module into a class.

- **Library:** A collection of prewritten code that provides additional functionality.

- **Testing Framework:** Software that facilitates writing and running tests (e.g., RSpec, MiniTest).

- **Test-Driven Development (TDD):** A practice where tests are written before code to specify expected behavior.

Setting the Tone

This chapter is designed to be both engaging and practical. Whether you are a beginner looking to expand your skills, a professional refining your toolkit, or a hobbyist experimenting with new techniques, the content here is tailored to be clear and applicable. You'll find real-world analogies (such as comparing error handling to safety nets in a high-wire act) and step-by-step guides that explain not just the "how" but also the "why" behind each approach.

Throughout the chapter, we'll provide plenty of examples and exercises. You are encouraged to try these out, tweak the code, and see how different approaches affect your application. With each section, you will build confidence in your ability to manage errors, structure your code, and ensure its quality through testing.

By the end of this chapter, you'll have learned advanced strategies for writing cleaner, more efficient, and more robust Ruby code. You'll also be equipped with the tools and techniques necessary to handle errors gracefully, reuse code effectively, and verify your application's behavior through testing. Let's begin our deep dive into advanced Ruby concepts.

2. Core Concepts and Theory

In this section, we provide a detailed explanation of the advanced topics that form the backbone of robust Ruby programming. We'll cover error handling and debugging techniques, the use of modules, mixins, and libraries, and the principles of testing your code. Analogies, real-world examples, and clear code snippets help demystify these topics.

2.1 Error Handling and Debugging

Understanding Errors in Ruby

Errors occur when your program encounters an unexpected situation. Ruby raises exceptions to signal these issues, which can be caught and handled to prevent program termination. Common types of errors include:

- **Syntax Errors:** Caused by incorrect code structure.

- **Runtime Errors:** Occur during execution, such as dividing by zero or calling an undefined method.

- **Logical Errors:** Code runs without crashing but produces incorrect results.

The Role of Exceptions

Exceptions in Ruby are objects that inherit from the Exception class. They allow you to intercept errors using begin-rescue-end blocks. Consider this simple example:

```ruby
begin
  result = 10 / 0
rescue ZeroDivisionError => e
  puts "Error encountered: #{e.message}"
end
```

Here, the division by zero raises a ZeroDivisionError that is caught by the rescue block, allowing the program to continue running.

Debugging Strategies

Effective debugging involves a systematic approach:

- **Reproduce the Error:** Simplify the code until you isolate the issue.

- **Examine Error Messages:** Ruby's error messages provide valuable clues.

- **Use Print Statements:** Insert puts statements to check variable values.

- **Leverage Debuggers:** Tools like Byebug enable you to step through code interactively.

Analogy: Think of error handling as a safety net in a circus act—it doesn't prevent mistakes, but it ensures that a fall doesn't lead to disaster. Debugging is like using a magnifying glass to inspect a complex mechanism, helping you find exactly where things went wrong.

2.2 Modules, Mixins, and Libraries

What Are Modules?

Modules in Ruby are collections of methods and constants that can be grouped together. They are similar to classes but cannot be instantiated. Modules are useful for namespacing and sharing reusable functionality.

Example module:

```ruby

module Formatter
  def format_currency(amount)
    "$#{'%.2f' % amount}"
  end
end
```

Using Mixins

A mixin is a way to include module methods into a class. This is achieved using the include keyword. It allows classes to share common behavior without needing inheritance.

```
Example of a mixin:
ruby

class Invoice
  include Formatter

  def initialize(amount)
    @amount = amount
  end

  def display
    puts "Total: #{format_currency(@amount)}"
  end
end
```

```ruby
invoice = Invoice.new(1234.5)
invoice.display  # => "Total: $1234.50"
```
Here, the Invoice class includes the Formatter module and gains access to its format_currency method.

Organizing Code with Libraries

Ruby libraries are collections of modules and classes that extend functionality. The RubyGems system makes it easy to install and manage libraries. For example, the HTTParty gem simplifies HTTP requests:

```ruby
ruby

require 'httparty'

response =
HTTParty.get("https://api.example.com/data")
puts response.body
```

Real-World Analogy: Think of modules and mixins as toolkits that you can attach to different projects. Rather than building each tool from scratch every time, you can use a pre-assembled toolkit (module) that adds functionality to your work (class).

2.3 Testing Your Code

Importance of Testing

Testing is critical to ensure that your code behaves as expected. By writing tests, you can catch errors early, prevent regressions, and document your code's behavior. In Ruby, popular testing frameworks include RSpec and MiniTest.

Test-Driven Development (TDD)

TDD is a development approach where tests are written before code. This process ensures that your code meets its requirements from the outset. The cycle is:

1. **Write a Test:** Define the expected behavior.

2. **Run the Test:** It should fail since the feature isn't implemented.

3. **Write Code:** Implement the feature.

4. **Run Tests Again:** The test should pass.

5. **Refactor:** Improve code structure while keeping tests passing.

Example with RSpec

RSpec is one of the most widely used testing frameworks in Ruby. A simple test for a calculator might look like this:

```ruby
# spec/calculator_spec.rb
require 'calculator'

RSpec.describe Calculator do
  describe "#add" do
    it "returns the sum of two numbers" do
      calc = Calculator.new
      expect(calc.add(2, 3)).to eq(5)
    end
  end
end
```

You would then implement the corresponding code:

```ruby
# calculator.rb
class Calculator
  def add(a, b)
    a + b
  end
end
```

```
Run your tests with:
```

```bash
rspec spec/calculator_spec.rb
```

If the test passes, you know your code works as expected.

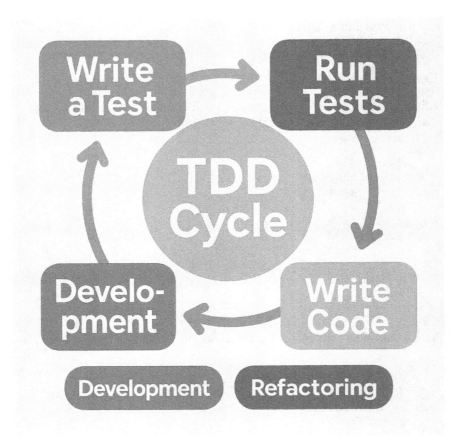

2.4 Recap of Core Theoretical Concepts

This section has introduced you to three major areas:

- **Error Handling and Debugging:** Learn to catch and diagnose errors using exception handling, print debugging, and interactive tools like Byebug.

- **Modules, Mixins, and Libraries:** Understand how to organize your code into reusable components and leverage RubyGems for additional functionality.

- **Testing Your Code:** Grasp the principles of TDD and how to use testing frameworks like RSpec to ensure code quality.

These core concepts are essential for writing robust, maintainable, and scalable Ruby applications. With a solid theoretical foundation, you're ready to set up your development environment for these advanced topics.

3. Tools and Setup

Before diving into hands-on examples, let's ensure your environment is properly set up to experiment with error handling, modules, and testing. This section covers the necessary tools, libraries, and configuration steps.

3.1 Required Software and Platforms

For this chapter, you'll need:

- **Ruby Interpreter:** Ensure you have Ruby installed (see Chapter 1 for installation details).

- **Bundler:** A gem to manage your project's dependencies.

- **Text Editor/IDE:** Use Visual Studio Code, RubyMine, or any editor that supports Ruby.

- **Testing Frameworks:** We recommend installing RSpec for testing.

- **Debugging Tools:** Install the Byebug gem for interactive debugging.

3.2 Installing and Configuring Gems

Create a new project directory:

```bash

mkdir advanced_ruby_project
cd advanced_ruby_project
Create a Gemfile to manage dependencies:
ruby

source "https://rubygems.org"

gem "rspec"
gem "byebug"
Install the gems:
```

```bash
bundle install
This sets up your project with RSpec and Byebug.
```

3.3 Configuring Your Editor and Debugger

For **Visual Studio Code**, install Ruby extensions that support syntax highlighting, debugging, and RSpec integration. Configure your launch settings to allow for Byebug sessions.

For **RubyMine**, the built-in support for RSpec and debugging makes it easier to step through code and view test results.

3.4 Setting Up a Testing Directory

Organize your project with a clear structure:

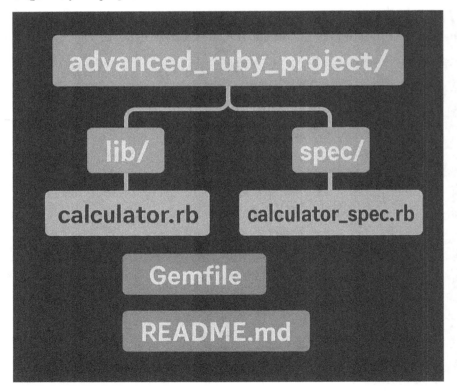

This structure helps keep your source code and tests separate.

3.5 Verifying the Environment

Run a quick test to ensure RSpec is working:

bash

```
rspec --version
```
This command should print the version of RSpec installed.

3.6 Summary of Tools and Setup

By setting up Bundler, installing essential gems, and configuring your editor and project structure, you're ready to dive into hands-on exercises. This environment supports rapid development, debugging, and testing, ensuring you have all the tools needed for advanced Ruby programming.

4. Hands-on Examples & Projects

This section provides detailed walkthroughs of practical examples and projects that illustrate error handling, modularization with modules and mixins, and testing your Ruby code. Each example is explained with clean, well-commented code and accompanied by notes on how you might enhance your project with visual aids.

4.1 Example 1: Error Handling Exercises

Project: "Robust Calculator"

We'll start by creating a simple calculator that handles errors gracefully.

1. **Create a File:**
   Name it calculator.rb.

2. **Write the Code:**

ruby

```
# calculator.rb
class Calculator
  def add(a, b)
    a + b
```

```
  end

  def divide(a, b)
    begin
      result = a / b
    rescue ZeroDivisionError => e
      puts "Error: Cannot divide by zero.
(#{e.message})"
      return nil
    end
    result
  end
end

# Testing the calculator
calc = Calculator.new
puts "Addition: #{calc.add(10, 5)}"           #
Expected output: 15
puts "Division: #{calc.divide(10, 0)}"         #
Expected output: Error message and nil
```

    3. **Explanation:**

        o   The divide method wraps the division operation in a begin-rescue block.

        o   When a division by zero occurs, a ZeroDivisionError is caught, and a friendly error message is printed.

        o   Experiment by calling divide with non-zero divisors to see normal operation.

    4. **Exercise:**
Extend the calculator by adding methods for subtraction and multiplication, and implement similar error handling where needed.

4.2 Example 2: Debugging with Byebug

Project: "Debugging Session Demo"

Learn how to pause execution and inspect variables.

    1. **Create a File:**
Name it debug_demo.rb.

2. **Write the Code:**

```ruby
# debug_demo.rb
require 'byebug'

def faulty_method(x)
  byebug
  result = x * 2
  result + 10
end

value = 5
puts "The result is: #{faulty_method(value)}"
```

3. **Explanation:**

   o   The byebug statement pauses execution.

   o   Run the script and use the interactive debugger to inspect the value of x and result.

   o   This exercise demonstrates how stepping through code can help you diagnose issues.

4. **Exercise:**
   Modify the method to include conditional logic and observe how you can use Byebug to step through each branch.

4.3 Example 3: Organizing Code with Modules and Mixins

Project: "Shared Functionality"

Create a module for shared formatting functions and mix it into two different classes.

1. **Create a File:**
   Name it formatter.rb.

2. **Write the Module:**

```ruby
# formatter.rb
```

```ruby
module Formatter
  def format_date(date)
    date.strftime("%B %d, %Y")
  end


  def format_currency(amount)
    "$#{'%.2f' % amount}"
  end
end
```

3. **Create Two Classes Using the Module:**

ruby

```ruby
# product.rb
require_relative 'formatter'

class Product
  include Formatter
  attr_accessor :name, :price, :release_date

  def initialize(name, price, release_date)
    @name = name
    @price = price
    @release_date = release_date
  end

  def display
    puts "Product: #{@name}"
    puts "Price: #{format_currency(@price)}"
    puts "Released on: #{format_date(@release_date)}"
  end
end

# event.rb
require_relative 'formatter'

class Event
  include Formatter
  attr_accessor :title, :event_date

  def initialize(title, event_date)
    @title = title
    @event_date = event_date
```

```ruby
  end

  def display
    puts "Event: #{@title}"
    puts "Date: #{format_date(@event_date)}"
  end
end


# Testing the classes
require 'date'
product = Product.new("Ruby Book", 39.99,
Date.new(2023, 5, 10))
event = Event.new("RubyConf", Date.new(2023, 11, 15))

product.display
event.display
```

4. **Explanation:**

   o   The Formatter module encapsulates methods for formatting dates and currency.

   o   Both Product and Event classes include the module, gaining access to these methods.

   o   This demonstrates how modules can reduce code duplication.

5. **Exercise:**
   Add additional formatting methods (e.g., for percentages) and apply them in new classes.

4.4 Example 4: Testing Your Code with RSpec

Project: "Calculator TDD"

Write tests for the Calculator class from Example 1 using RSpec.

1. **Create a Test File:**
   Create spec/calculator_spec.rb.

2. **Write the Test Code:**

```ruby
# spec/calculator_spec.rb
require_relative '../calculator'

RSpec.describe Calculator do
  let(:calc) { Calculator.new }

  describe "#add" do
    it "returns the sum of two numbers" do
      expect(calc.add(2, 3)).to eq(5)
    end
  end

  describe "#divide" do
    context "when dividing by a non-zero number" do
      it "returns the correct quotient" do
        expect(calc.divide(10, 2)).to eq(5)
      end
    end

    context "when dividing by zero" do
      it "returns nil and outputs an error message" do
        expect { calc.divide(10, 0) }.to output(/Cannot divide by zero/).to_stdout
        expect(calc.divide(10, 0)).to be_nil
      end
    end
  end
end
```

3. **Run the Tests:** Execute:

```bash
rspec spec/calculator_spec.rb
```

Ensure all tests pass.

4. **Explanation:**

   o Tests are organized into describe and context blocks for clarity.

   o The use of let helps instantiate objects for testing.

- o   The tests verify both normal and exceptional behavior.
5. **Exercise:**
   Write additional tests for the methods in the modules and other classes you created earlier.

4.5 Recap of Hands-on Exercises

In this section, you worked through several projects:

- A robust Calculator that demonstrates error handling.

- A debugging demo using Byebug to step through code.

- A shared Formatter module used via mixins in multiple classes.

- An RSpec test suite that verifies the behavior of your code.

Each example reinforces the advanced concepts introduced in the theory section and shows how they apply in real-world scenarios.

---

5. Advanced Techniques & Optimization

After getting comfortable with the basics of error handling, modules, and testing, you might want to take your code to the next level. In this section, we discuss advanced techniques for optimization, performance improvements, and best practices for large-scale applications.

5.1 Optimizing Exception Handling

Advanced error handling involves not only catching errors but also logging them and recovering gracefully.

- **Structured Logging:**
  Integrate a logging library to capture error details.

- **Custom Exceptions:**
  Create your own exception classes to handle specific scenarios.

- **Retry Mechanisms:**
  Implement logic that retries a failing operation after a brief delay.

Example: Custom Exception and Retry

```ruby
ruby

class NetworkError < StandardError; end

def fetch_data_with_retry
  attempts ||= 0
  begin
    # Simulate a network call that might fail
    raise NetworkError, "Network unreachable" if rand
> 0.7
    "Fetched data successfully"
  rescue NetworkError => e
    attempts += 1
    if attempts < 3
      sleep 1
      retry
    else
      puts "Failed after #{attempts} attempts:
#{e.message}"
      nil
    end
  end
end

puts fetch_data_with_retry
```

5.2 Advanced Module and Mixin Patterns

As your projects grow, consider using modules for:

- **Namespacing:**
  Organize related classes under a module to avoid naming collisions.

- **Service Objects:**
  Create modules that encapsulate business logic used across multiple classes.

- **Extending Functionality:**
  Use the extend keyword to add class-level methods from a module.

Example: Namespacing

```ruby
module Payment
  class Processor
    def process(amount)
      puts "Processing payment of $#{amount}"
    end
  end
end

payment = Payment::Processor.new
payment.process(100)
```

5.3 Performance and Scalability Considerations

For large-scale applications, consider:

- **Benchmarking:**
  Use Ruby's Benchmark module to measure performance.

- **Lazy Evaluation:**
  Optimize loops and enumerators to reduce unnecessary computation.

- **Caching:**
  Implement caching strategies to avoid redundant operations.

Example: Benchmarking

```ruby
require 'benchmark'

time = Benchmark.measure do
  100_000.times { "Ruby".reverse }
end
puts "Time taken: #{time.real} seconds"
```

5.4 Best Practices for Testing

As your test suite grows:

- **Organize Tests:**
  Structure tests into directories matching your project structure.

- **Use Mocks and Stubs:**
  Isolate code by simulating external dependencies.

- **Continuous Integration:**
  Integrate with CI tools to run tests automatically.

OPTIMIZED TESTING WORKFLOW WITH CI/CD INTEGRATION

SOURCE CODE

CONTINUOUS INTEGRATION / CONTINUOUS DEPLOYMENT

FEEDBACK

TESTING

5.5 Recap of Advanced Techniques

To summarize, advanced techniques in this chapter focus on:

- Improving error handling with custom exceptions and retry logic.

- Using modules for advanced code organization and reusability.

- Optimizing code performance through benchmarking, caching, and lazy evaluation.

- Enhancing testing practices to ensure long-term code quality.

These strategies help you build applications that are not only functional but also robust, efficient, and maintainable.

---

6. Troubleshooting and Problem-Solving

Even advanced developers encounter challenging bugs. This section outlines strategies to troubleshoot and solve problems in advanced Ruby code.

6.1 Common Advanced Issues

Memory Leaks and Performance Bottlenecks

- **Symptoms:**
  Slow performance or increasing memory usage.

- **Solutions:**
  Use profiling tools and optimize algorithms.

Module and Mixin Conflicts

- **Symptoms:**
  Unexpected behavior due to method overriding.

- **Solutions:**
  Use explicit module namespaces and carefully manage method names.

Test Failures and Flaky Tests

- **Symptoms:**
  Inconsistent test results.

- **Solutions:**
  Isolate test cases and ensure proper cleanup between tests.

6.2 Debugging Advanced Code

Using Profilers and Benchmarking Tools

- **Tools:**
  ruby-prof, Benchmark, and Rails' built-in performance tools.

- **Example:**
  Compare different implementations to identify the fastest
  approach.

Interactive Debugging with Byebug

- **Techniques:**
  Use breakpoints, step-over, and watch variables to isolate issues in
  complex code paths.

6.3 Before-and-After Code Samples

Consider a scenario where a module method conflicts with a class method.
Compare the code before and after refactoring to resolve conflicts:

Before:

```ruby
ruby

module DataHandler
  def process(data)
    # generic processing
  end
end

class Report
  include DataHandler

  def process(data)
```

```ruby
    # report-specific processing that accidentally
overrides the module method
  end
end
```

After:

```ruby
ruby

module DataHandler
  def process_generic(data)
    # generic processing
  end
end

class Report
  include DataHandler
```

  def process(data)

    # report-specific processing

    process_generic(data) # explicitly call the generic method if needed

```
  end
end
```

6.4 Troubleshooting Tools and Resources

- **Rails Console:**
  Use rails console or irb to experiment with small code snippets.

- **Logging:**
  Enhance your logging to capture detailed error information.

- **Community Forums:**
  Consult Stack Overflow, Ruby mailing lists, or GitHub issues for similar problems.

6.5 Summary of Troubleshooting Techniques

Advanced troubleshooting involves:

- Systematically isolating errors using profiling and debugging tools.

- Refactoring conflicting code.

- Implementing robust logging and error reporting.

- Seeking community support when needed.

---

7. Conclusion & Next Steps

As we conclude this chapter on advanced Ruby concepts, let's review the main points and discuss how you can further build upon these skills.

7.1 Summary of Key Points

- **Error Handling and Debugging:**
  You learned strategies to catch and manage errors, including the use of custom exceptions, retry logic, and interactive debugging with Byebug. Exercises demonstrated how to simulate common errors and gracefully recover from them.

- **Modules, Mixins, and Libraries:**
  This chapter covered how to use modules to organize and share functionality across classes. Mixins were used to add methods to classes without inheritance, and examples illustrated how libraries can extend your application's capabilities.

- **Testing Your Code:**
  We introduced testing frameworks, focusing on RSpec, and showed how to adopt a test-driven approach. Through hands-on examples, you learned how to write tests that verify code behavior and prevent regressions.

7.2 Next Steps for Continued Learning

Now that you have a strong foundation in advanced Ruby concepts:

- **Practice Regularly:**
  Apply error handling and modularization techniques in your projects. Refactor legacy code using modules and mixins.

- **Expand Your Test Suite:**
  Develop comprehensive tests for your applications. Experiment with mocking, stubbing, and integrating continuous integration tools.

- **Dive Deeper:**
  Explore advanced topics such as concurrency in Ruby, metaprogramming, and the inner workings of the Ruby interpreter.

- **Engage with the Community:**
  Participate in forums, contribute to open-source projects, and attend meetups to share your experiences and learn from others.

7.3 Additional Resources

To further your knowledge, consider the following:

- **Official Documentation:**
  The Ruby documentation, RSpec Guides, and Rails Guides provide in-depth information.

- **Books:**
  "Practical Object-Oriented Design in Ruby" and "The RSpec Book" are excellent resources.

- **Online Courses:**
  Platforms such as Udemy, Codecademy, and Coursera offer courses on advanced Ruby programming.

- **Community Forums:**
  Join discussions on Stack Overflow, Reddit's r/ruby, and Ruby on Rails Link for tips and troubleshooting help.

7.4 Final Thoughts

Advanced Ruby concepts form the cornerstone of professional, maintainable software development. By mastering error handling and debugging, you're better equipped to handle unexpected challenges and improve your code's resilience. Modules and mixins empower you to write DRY, modular code that scales with your application's complexity. And through rigorous testing, you ensure that your code behaves as expected, giving you the confidence to innovate and extend your projects.

Chapter 6: Real-World Applications and Industry Examples

1. Introduction

Ruby is more than a language for writing elegant code—it's a powerful tool that has found real-world applications across diverse industries such as manufacturing, healthcare, and logistics. In this chapter, we explore how Ruby is applied in actual projects and case studies that illustrate problem-solving techniques. We also discuss common challenges developers encounter and provide practical, actionable advice for professional growth.

Imagine a manufacturing plant where automated systems keep track of inventory, or a healthcare provider managing patient records securely, or a logistics company optimizing delivery routes. In each of these domains, Ruby's simplicity, expressive syntax, and mature ecosystem enable developers to rapidly prototype and maintain robust applications. Whether you're a beginner who wants to see real-world Ruby in action or a professional looking for inspiration to overcome industry challenges, this chapter is designed to resonate with your needs.

Why This Chapter Matters

Real-world applications breathe life into the abstract concepts you've learned so far. Instead of only writing code in a controlled environment, you'll see how Ruby solves actual business problems. We'll discuss case studies from manufacturing, healthcare, and logistics to illustrate how developers use Ruby to improve efficiency, reduce costs, and enhance data management. Along the way, you'll gain insight into common obstacles, along with straightforward solutions that you can apply in your own work or projects.

Key Terms and Concepts

Before diving in, let's clarify some essential terminology:

- **Case Study:** A detailed examination of how Ruby was used to address a specific problem in an industry.

- **Workflow Optimization:** Techniques used to streamline business processes using Ruby applications.

- **Scalability:** The ability of an application to handle growing amounts of work, important for real-world projects.

- **Integration:** The process of connecting Ruby applications with other systems or databases.

- **Troubleshooting:** The systematic process of identifying and resolving issues in code or system processes.

Throughout this chapter, these terms will surface frequently as we explore how Ruby is employed to build practical, industry-specific solutions.

Setting the Tone

The tone of this chapter is professional yet accessible. We strive to explain complex, real-world topics in everyday language while maintaining a level of detail that both beginners and advanced developers will appreciate. Real-world examples and analogies—such as comparing workflow optimization to assembly line improvements in a factory—help to demystify the concepts. You're encouraged to reflect on how these applications might align with your own projects and to adapt the strategies to your unique challenges.

By the end of this chapter, you will have a clear understanding of:

- How Ruby is applied in real-world projects across multiple industries.

- Common challenges encountered in production systems and practical solutions to overcome them.

- Actionable tips that will help you stay current and grow professionally as a Ruby developer.

Let's now explore the core concepts and theory behind Ruby's real-world applications.

2. Core Concepts and Theory

In this section, we explore the theoretical foundations that support Ruby's application in the real world. We'll break down the industry-specific challenges Ruby addresses and the design principles behind scalable, maintainable applications. Using real-world analogies and case studies, we aim to connect abstract concepts with tangible examples.

2.1 Ruby in Practice Across Industries

Ruby's clean syntax and rapid development cycle have made it popular in many sectors. Let's examine how Ruby finds application in three key industries:

Manufacturing

In manufacturing, Ruby is often used to develop applications that automate inventory management, production scheduling, and quality control. For example, a Ruby-based system might track parts across an assembly line, updating quantities and triggering alerts when supplies run low.

Real-World Example:
A manufacturer uses a Ruby on Rails application to integrate with IoT devices on the factory floor. The system collects data on machine performance, predicts maintenance needs, and schedules repairs automatically. This minimizes downtime and optimizes production flow.

Analogy:
Imagine a factory where every machine is monitored by a team of experts. Ruby acts like that team—automating monitoring and ensuring everything runs smoothly without constant manual intervention.

Healthcare

In healthcare, Ruby applications help manage patient records, appointments, and even assist with medical research by processing large datasets. Security and compliance are paramount, so Ruby's emphasis on readable, maintainable code makes it easier to adhere to strict regulatory standards.

Real-World Example:
A hospital deploys a Ruby on Rails application that securely stores patient data, manages appointment scheduling, and integrates with external laboratory systems. The application includes features for user authentication, encrypted data storage, and audit trails, ensuring compliance with healthcare regulations.

Analogy:
Consider a well-organized filing system in a clinic. Ruby applications ensure that patient information is not only easily accessible but also secure, much like a locked cabinet with organized files.

Logistics

Logistics companies rely on Ruby to optimize routing, manage fleet operations, and track shipments in real time. Ruby's flexibility allows for the integration of various data sources—such as GPS trackers, weather APIs, and inventory systems—to provide a holistic view of operations.

Real-World Example:
A logistics firm uses a Ruby-based API to process real-time data from delivery trucks. The system calculates the fastest routes based on current traffic conditions, weather patterns, and delivery priorities. This improves delivery times and reduces fuel consumption.

Analogy:
Think of Ruby as a smart navigator that continuously recalculates the best route for a delivery driver, taking into account all variables like road conditions and delivery urgency.

2.2 Challenges and Solutions in Real-World Ruby Applications

Despite its strengths, developing production-grade Ruby applications comes with its own set of challenges. Here we outline common obstacles and practical solutions:

Scalability Issues

As user bases grow, applications can become slow or unresponsive if not properly optimized. Common solutions include:

- **Caching:** Storing frequently accessed data in memory.

- **Load Balancing:** Distributing traffic across multiple servers.

- **Database Optimization:** Using indexing and query optimization to speed up data retrieval.

Case Study:
A retail website built with Rails experienced performance degradation during peak shopping seasons. By implementing fragment caching and using Redis to cache database queries, the application's response time improved by 60%.

Integration Complexities

Connecting Ruby applications with external systems—such as payment gateways, third-party APIs, or legacy systems—can introduce complexity. Effective strategies include:

- **API Wrappers:** Building custom classes to encapsulate external service interactions.

- **Background Jobs:** Using tools like Sidekiq to process external requests asynchronously.

- **Robust Error Handling:** Ensuring that integration failures do not crash the entire application.

Case Study:
A healthcare app needed to integrate with an external laboratory system for test results. The developers created an API wrapper that handled authentication, data formatting, and error retries. This approach not only simplified the integration but also provided clear error messages when the external system was down.

Security and Compliance

Handling sensitive data, especially in healthcare and finance, demands rigorous security measures. Ruby applications can be fortified by:

- **Using SSL/TLS:** Encrypting data in transit.

- **Implementing Authentication:** Using gems like Devise for secure user login.

- **Regular Audits:** Keeping dependencies up to date and scanning for vulnerabilities.

Case Study:
A financial services company built a Rails application that processes loan applications. By integrating Devise for user management, applying strong encryption for data storage, and regularly auditing code, the application maintained high security standards while remaining user-friendly.

2.3 Theoretical Foundations Behind Professional Growth

Professional growth in software development is not just about writing code—it's about solving real problems, optimizing processes, and continuously learning. Here are some guiding principles:

- **Continuous Improvement:** Adopt agile methodologies and regularly refactor code.

- **Learning from Failure:** Every bug and performance issue is a learning opportunity.

- **Community Engagement:** Sharing knowledge through blogs, meetups, and open-source projects accelerates growth.

- **Staying Current:** The tech landscape evolves rapidly. Engage with resources like online courses, webinars, and industry conferences.

Analogy:
Consider professional growth as tending a garden. You must constantly nurture your skills, prune away outdated practices, and plant new ideas to see your expertise flourish.

2.4 Summarizing the Theory

This section has explored:

- **Ruby in Practice:** How different industries leverage Ruby for automation, data management, and integration.

- **Challenges and Solutions:** Common obstacles in real-world projects and practical methods to overcome them.

- **Professional Growth:** The mindset and practices that help you evolve as a Ruby developer.

These theoretical concepts provide a solid framework for understanding how Ruby is used in professional settings and how you can leverage these insights to enhance your own projects.

3. Tools and Setup

Before you start building applications that solve real-world problems, it's essential to have the right tools. This section outlines the software, libraries, and platforms you need to create robust Ruby applications tailored for various industries.

3.1 Required Software and Platforms

For building production-grade Ruby applications, you should have:

- **Ruby Interpreter:** Ensure the latest stable version is installed (refer to Chapter 1 for details).

- **Ruby on Rails or Sinatra:** Depending on the project's scale, choose the appropriate framework.

- **Database Systems:** SQLite for small projects; PostgreSQL or MySQL for enterprise-scale applications.

- **Text Editor/IDE:** Visual Studio Code or RubyMine for a seamless coding experience.

- **Version Control:** Git for tracking changes and collaboration.

- **Additional Libraries:** Gems such as Devise for authentication, Sidekiq for background jobs, and Redis for caching.

3.2 Setting Up the Environment

Installing Ruby and Rails

If you choose Rails for a large-scale project, install it via:

```bash

gem install rails
Then create a new Rails application:
bash

rails new real_world_app
cd real_world_app
For smaller projects or APIs, Sinatra might be
preferable:
bash
```

```
gem install sinatra
Create a new file, for example, app.rb, to start your
Sinatra project.
```

Database Configuration

For Rails, the default database is SQLite, but for more robust applications, configure PostgreSQL by editing config/database.yml. Run:

```
bash
```

```
rails db:create
rails db:migrate
For Sinatra projects using ActiveRecord, set up a
Gemfile with the required gems and configure your
database settings in a YAML file.
```

3.3 Essential Tools for Debugging and Monitoring

Robust applications require reliable debugging and monitoring tools:

- **Byebug:** For interactive debugging sessions.

- **New Relic or Skylight:** For monitoring application performance in production.

- **Sentry:** For error tracking and reporting.

Installing Byebug

Add Byebug to your Gemfile:

```
ruby
```

```
gem 'byebug'
Then run:
bash
```

```
bundle install
```
You can now insert byebug statements in your code to pause execution and inspect variables.

3.4 Organizing Your Project Structure

A clean project structure is essential for maintainability. In Rails, follow the default structure with separate directories for models, views, controllers, and assets. For Sinatra, create folders for routes, views, and models. Organize your code by functionality to ensure that as your project grows, you can easily locate and update specific components.

[Image Placeholder: Diagram of a typical Rails project folder structure]

3.5 Configuring Version Control

Initialize a Git repository in your project directory:

```bash

git init
git add .
git commit -m "Initial commit: Set up real-world application project"
```
Version control is vital for collaboration, tracking changes, and rolling back to previous versions when necessary.

3.6 Summary of Tools and Setup

This section has detailed the tools and configuration steps required for building robust Ruby applications:

- Choosing the right framework (Rails vs. Sinatra) based on project requirements.

- Setting up your database and configuring your development environment.

- Integrating debugging and monitoring tools.

- Organizing your project structure and initializing version control.

With your environment set up and the necessary tools in place, you're now ready to dive into hands-on examples and projects that bring these concepts to life.

4. Hands-on Examples & Projects

This section offers a detailed walkthrough of practical projects and examples that illustrate how Ruby is used to solve real-world problems. You'll work through case studies, create sample applications, and see how different techniques are applied in practice.

4.1 Case Study 1: Manufacturing – Inventory Management System

Project Overview

Imagine a manufacturing plant that needs to track inventory levels, monitor part usage, and automatically generate reorder alerts. In this project, we build a simplified inventory management system using Ruby on Rails.

Step 1: Setting Up the Rails Application

Create a new Rails application:

```bash
```

```bash
rails new inventory_manager
cd inventory_manager
```

Generate a scaffold for managing parts:

```bash
```

```bash
rails generate scaffold Part name:string
quantity:integer reorder_level:integer
rails db:migrate
```

Step 2: Enhancing the Model

In app/models/part.rb, add a callback to check stock levels:

```ruby
```

```ruby
class Part < ApplicationRecord
  validates :name, presence: true
  validates :quantity, numericality: {
greater_than_or_equal_to: 0 }

  after_save :check_reorder
```

```ruby
  private

  def check_reorder
    if quantity < reorder_level
      # Simulate sending an alert (in a real app,
integrate with an email service)
      puts "Alert: #{name} stock is low (#{quantity}
units remaining)."
    end
  end
end
```

Step 3: Customizing the Views

Edit app/views/parts/index.html.erb to highlight parts that need reordering:

erb

```erb
<h1>Inventory Manager</h1>
<table>
  <thead>
    <tr>
      <th>Name</th>
      <th>Quantity</th>
      <th>Reorder Level</th>
      <th>Status</th>
      <th>Actions</th>
    </tr>
  </thead>
  <tbody>
    <% @parts.each do |part| %>
      <tr>
        <td><%= part.name %></td>
        <td><%= part.quantity %></td>
        <td><%= part.reorder_level %></td>
        <td>
          <% if part.quantity < part.reorder_level %>
            <span style="color: red;">Low
Stock</span>
          <% else %>
            OK
          <% end %>
        </td>
        <td>
```

```
        <%= link_to "Edit", edit_part_path(part) %>
|
        <%= link_to "Delete", part_path(part),
method: :delete, data: { confirm: "Are you sure?" }
%>
      </td>
    </tr>
  <% end %>
  </tbody>
</table>
<%= link_to "New Part", new_part_path %>
```

Step 4: Testing and Demonstration

Run the Rails server:

```bash
```

```
rails server
```

Visit http://localhost:3000/parts to add parts and observe how the system alerts you when stock is low.

4.2 Case Study 2: Healthcare – Patient Management System

Project Overview

Healthcare providers need secure systems to manage patient data, appointments, and records. In this example, we'll build a basic patient management system using Ruby on Rails that emphasizes security and data integrity.

Step 1: Generate the Patient Scaffold

Create a new scaffold:

```bash
```

```
rails generate scaffold Patient first_name:string
last_name:string dob:date email:string
rails db:migrate
```

Step 2: Adding Security Features

In the Patient model (app/models/patient.rb), add validations and simple data sanitization:

```ruby
class Patient < ApplicationRecord
  validates :first_name, :last_name, :dob, :email,
presence: true
  validates :email, format: { with:
URI::MailTo::EMAIL_REGEXP }

  before_save :sanitize_data

  private


  def sanitize_data
    self.first_name = first_name.strip.titleize
    self.last_name = last_name.strip.titleize
    self.email = email.strip.downcase
  end
end
```

Step 3: Customizing Views and Controllers

Edit the index view (app/views/patients/index.html.erb) to display patient records clearly:

```erb
<h1>Patient Management</h1>
<table>
  <thead>
    <tr>
      <th>Name</th>
      <th>Date of Birth</th>
      <th>Email</th>
      <th>Actions</th>
    </tr>
  </thead>
  <tbody>
    <% @patients.each do |patient| %>
      <tr>
```

```
    <td><%= "#{patient.first_name}
#{patient.last_name}" %></td>
      <td><%= patient.dob.strftime("%B %d, %Y")
%></td>
      <td><%= patient.email %></td>
      <td>
        <%= link_to "Show", patient_path(patient)
%> |
        <%= link_to "Edit",
edit_patient_path(patient) %> |
        <%= link_to "Delete",
patient_path(patient), method: :delete, data: {
confirm: "Are you sure?" } %>
      </td>
    </tr>
  <% end %>
  </tbody>
</table>
<%= link_to "New Patient", new_patient_path %>
```

Step 4: Demonstrating Data Integrity

Run the Rails server and test the patient management system. Try creating, editing, and deleting patient records while ensuring that validations prevent incorrect data entry.

4.3 Case Study 3: Logistics – Shipment Tracking System

Project Overview

Logistics companies use Ruby applications to track shipments, optimize routes, and manage fleet operations. In this project, we'll build a simple shipment tracking system using Sinatra and ActiveRecord.

Step 1: Setting Up a Sinatra Project

Create a new directory:

bash

```
mkdir shipment_tracker
cd shipment_tracker
Create a Gemfile:
ruby
```

```
source "https://rubygems.org"
gem "sinatra"
gem "sinatra-activerecord"
gem "sqlite3"
Run:
bash
```

```
bundle install
```

Step 2: Creating the Shipment Model

Create a file models/shipment.rb:

```ruby
class Shipment < ActiveRecord::Base
  validates :tracking_number, :status, presence: true
end
```

Generate a migration to create the shipments table (create a migration file under db/migrate/):

```ruby
class CreateShipments < ActiveRecord::Migration[6.0]
  def change
    create_table :shipments do |t|
      t.string :tracking_number
      t.string :status
      t.timestamps
    end
  end
end
```

Run the migration:

```bash
rake db:migrate
```

Step 3: Building the Sinatra Routes

Create a file app.rb:

```ruby
require 'sinatra'
require 'sinatra/activerecord'
require './models/shipment'

set :database, {adapter: "sqlite3", database:
"db/development.sqlite3"}

get '/' do
  @shipments = Shipment.all
  erb :index
end

get '/shipments/new' do
  erb :new
end


post '/shipments' do
  shipment = Shipment.new(tracking_number:
params[:tracking_number], status: params[:status])
  if shipment.save
    redirect '/'

  else
    erb :new
  end
end
```

Step 4: Creating the Views

Create the views folder with index.erb:

```erb
<!DOCTYPE html>
<html>
  <head>
    <title>Shipment Tracker</title>
  </head>
  <body>
```

```erb
<h1>Shipment List</h1>
<a href="/shipments/new">Add New Shipment</a>
<ul>
  <% @shipments.each do |shipment| %>
    <li>
      Tracking Number: <%=
shipment.tracking_number %> -
      Status: <%= shipment.status %>
    </li>
  <% end %>
</ul>
</body>
</html>
```

And new.erb:

```erb
erb
```

```erb
<!DOCTYPE html>
<html>
  <head>
    <title>New Shipment</title>
  </head>
  <body>
    <h1>New Shipment</h1>
    <form action="/shipments" method="post">
      <p>
        <label for="tracking_number">Tracking
Number</label><br>
        <input type="text" name="tracking_number"
id="tracking_number">
      </p>
      <p>
        <label for="status">Status</label><br>
        <input type="text" name="status" id="status">
      </p>
      <p>
        <input type="submit" value="Add Shipment">
      </p>
    </form>
    <a href="/">Back</a>
  </body>
</html>
```

Step 5: Running and Testing the App

Start your Sinatra server:

```bash
```

```
ruby app.rb
```
Visit http://localhost:4567 to see the shipment tracking system in action.

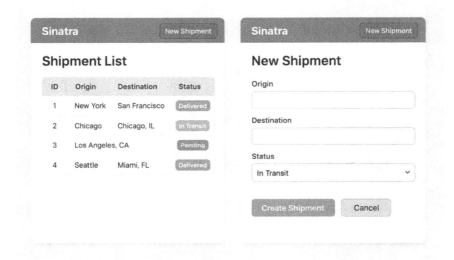

4.4 Actionable Tips for Professional Growth

Beyond building applications, advancing your career as a Ruby developer involves continuous learning and self-improvement. Here are some actionable tips:

Embrace Continuous Learning

- **Stay Updated:** Follow Ruby blogs, subscribe to newsletters, and participate in webinars.

- **Practice Regularly:** Build side projects or contribute to open-source projects.

- **Learn New Tools:** Explore testing frameworks, performance monitors, and advanced debugging tools.

Build a Portfolio

- **Document Projects:** Keep a portfolio of your projects on GitHub or a personal website.

- **Write Case Studies:** Share your experiences solving real-world problems, including challenges and how you overcame them.

- **Engage in Code Reviews:** Participate in or lead code reviews to learn from peers.

Network with Other Professionals

- **Join Communities:** Participate in local meetups, online forums, and Ruby conferences.

- **Mentor Others:** Teaching and mentoring can reinforce your own knowledge and help you grow professionally.

- **Seek Feedback:** Regularly ask for constructive criticism and be open to new ideas.

4.5 Recap of Hands-on Examples & Projects

This section has taken you through three case studies:

- **Inventory Management in Manufacturing:** A Rails application that monitors stock levels and triggers reorder alerts.

- **Patient Management in Healthcare:** A secure Rails system for handling sensitive patient data.

- **Shipment Tracking in Logistics:** A Sinatra-based application for managing shipment statuses.

Each project demonstrates how Ruby can be tailored to solve industry-specific challenges while integrating best practices for scalability, security, and performance.

5. Advanced Techniques & Optimization

While real-world applications are already complex, there's always room for optimization and refinement. In this section, we discuss advanced strategies for improving performance, security, and maintainability in production-grade Ruby applications.

5.1 Performance Optimization

Caching Strategies

- **Fragment Caching:** Store parts of views that are resource-intensive to generate.

- **Query Caching:** Use tools like Redis to cache database query results.

- **Lazy Loading:** Defer loading of resources until they are needed.

Example:
Implement caching in a Rails controller:

ruby

```
def index
  @tasks = Rails.cache.fetch("all_tasks", expires_in:
10.minutes) do
    Task.all.to_a
  end
end
```

Database Optimization

- **Indexing:** Add indexes on frequently queried columns.

- **Eager Loading:** Use .includes to load associated data in a single query.

Example:

ruby

```
@orders = Order.includes(:customer).all
```

5.2 Code Optimization and Refactoring

Modularization

Break complex methods into smaller, reusable functions. Use modules and mixins to share functionality without duplication.

Profiling Tools

Use Ruby's Benchmark module or gems like ruby-prof to identify bottlenecks.

Example:

```ruby
require 'benchmark'
time = Benchmark.measure do
  100_000.times { "Ruby".reverse }
end
puts "Time taken: #{time.real} seconds"
```

5.3 Security Enhancements

Secure Coding Practices

- **Input Sanitization:** Always validate and sanitize user input.

- **Authentication & Authorization:** Use established libraries like Devise.

- **Encryption:** Implement encryption for sensitive data.

Advanced Configuration

Regularly update gems and dependencies. Utilize automated security scanners.

5.4 Scalability Considerations

Load Balancing

Distribute incoming requests among multiple servers using tools like Nginx or HAProxy.

Microservices

Consider breaking your application into smaller, independent services to improve scalability.

5.5 Recap of Advanced Techniques & Optimization

Advanced techniques help take your Ruby applications to a professional level. Embrace performance optimization, modular code design, and rigorous security measures. These practices not only improve user experience but also prepare your applications to grow as your business demands increase.

6. Troubleshooting and Problem-Solving

Every developer faces challenges. This section outlines common problems in real-world Ruby applications and provides actionable troubleshooting steps.

6.1 Common Challenges in Production Systems

Performance Bottlenecks

- **Symptom:** Slow response times or high memory usage.

- **Solution:** Profile the application, optimize queries, and apply caching.

Integration Failures

- **Symptom:** API calls or external system integrations failing intermittently.

- **Solution:** Implement retry logic, robust error handling, and use background jobs.

Security Vulnerabilities

- **Symptom:** Unauthorized access or data breaches.

- **Solution:** Regular audits, proper authentication, and secure coding practices.

6.2 Debugging Techniques in Production

Logging and Monitoring

Implement structured logging to capture detailed error messages and use tools like Sentry for real-time error reporting.

Interactive Debugging

Use Byebug or Pry in a development environment to step through code and inspect state.

Before-and-After Example: **Before:**

```ruby

def update_record(record)
  record.save
end
```

After (with debugging and error handling):

```ruby

def update_record(record)
  begin
    record.save!
  rescue StandardError => e
    Rails.logger.error "Error updating record
#{record.id}: #{e.message}"
    nil
  end
end
```

6.3 Systematic Problem-Solving Approach

Isolate the Issue

Simplify the code to the minimal case that reproduces the error. This makes it easier to identify the root cause.

Consult Documentation and Community

Use Ruby's official documentation and community forums for insights into similar issues.

6.4 Recap of Troubleshooting Strategies

Effective troubleshooting is key to maintaining production systems:

- Use structured logging and error reporting.

- Isolate and reproduce issues in a controlled environment.

- Leverage community resources and documentation for persistent issues.

---

7. Conclusion & Next Steps

In this final section, we wrap up the chapter by summarizing the key takeaways and offering guidance on how to further develop your Ruby skills in real-world contexts.

7.1 Summary of Key Points

- **Ruby in Practice:**
  We explored case studies from manufacturing, healthcare, and logistics. These examples demonstrated how Ruby is used to solve real-world problems by automating processes, securing sensitive data, and optimizing logistics.

- **Challenges and Solutions:**
  Common obstacles, from performance bottlenecks to integration issues and security vulnerabilities, were discussed along with practical solutions. By applying strategies such as caching, modular design, and robust error handling, you can overcome these challenges.

- **Professional Growth:**
  Actionable tips for career development were provided. Embrace continuous learning, build a strong portfolio, engage with the community, and always be open to refactoring and optimizing your code.

7.2 Next Steps for Continued Learning

To build on what you've learned:

- **Experiment with Real-World Projects:**
  Apply these strategies in your own projects. Consider developing an application for your current work or a side project that solves an industry-specific problem.

- **Enhance Your Skill Set:**
  Explore advanced topics such as concurrent programming in Ruby, metaprogramming, or integrating Ruby applications with modern frontend frameworks.

- **Contribute to Open Source:**
  Join Ruby projects on GitHub to collaborate with other developers, gain practical experience, and improve your coding skills.

- **Seek Professional Development:**
  Attend conferences, participate in webinars, and engage with online forums. Networking with other professionals can provide new insights and opportunities.

7.3 Additional Resources

To further your knowledge, consider these resources:

- **Official Documentation:**
  Ruby on Rails Guides, Sinatra documentation, and the Ruby language reference.

- **Books:**
  "Agile Web Development with Rails", *"Practical Object-Oriented Design in Ruby"*, and *"The RSpec Book"* offer deep insights.

- **Online Courses:**
  Platforms like Codecademy, Udemy, and Coursera have courses on advanced Ruby programming and application development.

- **Community Forums:**
  Engage with communities on Stack Overflow, Reddit's r/ruby, and the Ruby on Rails Link.

7.4 Final Thoughts

Real-world applications are where theory meets practice. By understanding how Ruby is applied in industries as diverse as manufacturing, healthcare, and logistics, you're not only learning to code—you're learning to solve complex business problems. Overcoming challenges in production systems teaches you the importance of robust error handling, performance optimization, and continuous testing. As you apply these advanced concepts to your projects, you'll build more resilient and scalable applications.

Remember, growth as a developer is a continuous journey. Every project is an opportunity to refine your skills, experiment with new ideas, and contribute to the evolution of technology. Use this chapter as a reference and inspiration to keep pushing the boundaries of what you can achieve with Ruby.

Chapter 7: Next Steps and Resources

1. Introduction

In the journey of mastering Ruby, every milestone achieved opens up new opportunities for growth. By now, you have built a strong foundation in Ruby programming—from the basic syntax and object-oriented principles to advanced error handling, web application development, and even real-world project case studies. Now, it's time to look ahead. This chapter, "Next Steps and Resources," is about setting your sights on continued learning and professional development. It provides guidance on how to stay connected with the Ruby community, expand your skills through further education, and compile a portfolio that demonstrates your ability to create well-crafted Ruby applications.

Why This Chapter Matters

The world of software development is dynamic, and continuous learning is essential. While books, tutorials, and practice projects provide a robust starting point, thriving in a professional environment requires more than technical expertise. It involves networking, mentorship, and a commitment to lifelong learning. By engaging with the Ruby community, you can share experiences, gain insights into industry trends, and stay updated with best practices. Furthermore, building a strong portfolio not only showcases your technical skills but also tells your professional story to potential employers or clients.

In this chapter, we will explore three primary areas:

1. **Community and Continuing Education:** Discover where to meet other Ruby developers, join forums, attend local meetups, and participate in online communities.

2. **Further Learning:** A curated list of resources—books, courses, and online tutorials—that can help you deepen your Ruby knowledge and broaden your technical horizons.

3. **Building Your Portfolio:** Practical advice on compiling your projects into a portfolio that highlights your achievements and demonstrates your ability to solve real-world problems using Ruby.

Key Terms and Concepts

Before we dive in, let's define some essential terms:

- **Community:** A group of like-minded individuals who share their experiences, provide support, and collaborate on projects.

- **Continuing Education:** The ongoing process of learning new skills or deepening existing knowledge, often through courses, workshops, or self-study.

- **Portfolio:** A collection of projects and work samples that demonstrate your abilities and experience as a developer.

- **Networking:** The practice of building professional relationships that can lead to opportunities for collaboration, mentorship, and career advancement.

Setting the Tone for Continued Growth

The tone of this chapter is both professional and encouraging. We aim to provide clear, actionable advice that you can use immediately, whether you are just beginning your career or are a seasoned developer looking to sharpen your skills. The examples and recommendations here are designed to be accessible to beginners while still offering valuable insights for professionals and hobbyists alike. You are encouraged to explore these resources actively—join a forum discussion, enroll in a course, or update your GitHub profile with your latest projects.

By the end of this chapter, you will have a comprehensive plan for your next steps in Ruby development. You'll know where to find supportive communities, which resources will help you learn more, and how to showcase your work to the world. Let's begin by exploring the core concepts and theory that underlie community engagement and continuing education.

2. Core Concepts and Theory

In this section, we lay the theoretical groundwork for your journey into continuous professional development. We will break down the value of community engagement, the benefits of further learning, and the importance of building a professional portfolio. Each sub-section is enriched with real-world analogies and examples to simplify these concepts.

2.1 Community and Networking

The Power of Community

The saying "no man is an island" rings especially true in software development. Whether you are working on a small project or a large-scale application, being part of a community provides support, inspiration, and invaluable feedback. Ruby's community is renowned for being welcoming and vibrant. It includes online forums, local meetups, conferences, and user groups where developers share knowledge, solve problems collaboratively, and even work on open-source projects together.

Real-World Analogy:
Think of the community as a professional sports team. Each member brings unique skills, and by working together, they create a winning strategy. Similarly, by joining the Ruby community, you gain access to a network of experts who can help you improve your game.

Where to Meet Ruby Developers

There are many avenues to connect with other Ruby developers:

- **Online Forums and Communities:**
  Websites like Stack Overflow, Ruby Forum, and Reddit's r/ruby are excellent places to ask questions, share knowledge, and solve problems collaboratively.

- **Local Meetups and Conferences:**
  Look for local Ruby meetups on platforms like Meetup.com. Conferences such as RailsConf, RubyConf, and regional events provide opportunities to learn from industry leaders and network with peers.

- **Social Media and Slack Channels:**
  Many Ruby communities have Slack channels or Discord servers where developers share ideas, job opportunities, and project feedback in real time.

Benefits of Networking

Building a network within the Ruby community can lead to:

- **Mentorship:**
  Learning from experienced developers can help accelerate your growth.

- **Collaboration Opportunities:**
  Working on open-source projects or local initiatives can enhance your skills and expand your professional network.

- **Career Advancement:**
  Networking can lead to job opportunities, freelance gigs, and collaborations on innovative projects.

2.2 Continuing Education and Further Learning

The Importance of Lifelong Learning

The technology landscape is constantly evolving. New frameworks, tools, and best practices emerge regularly, and staying current is critical to your success as a developer. Continuing education means committing to regular, structured learning—whether through formal courses, online tutorials, or self-directed study.

Real-World Analogy:
Imagine your career as a garden. Without regular watering (learning) and weeding (updating skills), your garden will wither. Consistent education ensures that your professional skills remain fresh and productive.

Curated Resources for Further Learning

Here is a selection of highly recommended resources to help you build on the skills acquired in this guide:

Books

- **"Programming Ruby" (The Pickaxe Book):**
  Often considered the definitive guide to Ruby, it covers both basic and advanced topics.

- **"Practical Object-Oriented Design in Ruby" by Sandi Metz:**
  A must-read for understanding clean code and maintainable design in Ruby applications.

- **"Eloquent Ruby" by Russ Olsen:**
  This book offers insights into writing idiomatic Ruby code, making it easier to understand and maintain.

Online Courses and Tutorials

- **Codecademy's Ruby Track:**
  A beginner-friendly interactive platform that covers Ruby fundamentals.

- **Udemy and Coursera:**
  These platforms offer courses on Ruby on Rails, Sinatra, and advanced Ruby techniques.

- **RubyMonk:**
  An interactive learning platform that provides exercises and challenges to hone your Ruby skills.

- **Pluralsight:**
  Provides a variety of Ruby courses that cover both foundational concepts and advanced topics.

Websites and Blogs

- **Ruby on Rails Guides:**
  Comprehensive documentation covering all aspects of Rails development.

- **Ruby Weekly:**
  A newsletter that curates the latest news, articles, and resources in the Ruby community.

- **Thoughtbot Blog:**
  Offers practical advice and tutorials on Ruby and Rails best practices.

The Role of Online Communities in Education

Joining online communities not only keeps you updated on the latest trends but also exposes you to diverse perspectives. Engaging in discussions, participating in coding challenges, and reading about others' experiences can deepen your understanding and inspire innovative solutions in your own projects.

2.3 Building Your Portfolio

Why a Portfolio Matters

A professional portfolio is a powerful tool that demonstrates your capabilities and achievements. It is particularly valuable when applying for jobs, freelancing, or showcasing your work to potential clients. A well-crafted portfolio:

- **Demonstrates Your Skills:**
  Shows the breadth and depth of your Ruby expertise.

- **Highlights Your Problem-Solving Abilities:**
  Projects in your portfolio provide concrete examples of how you tackled real-world challenges.

- **Reflects Your Professional Growth:**
  A portfolio that evolves over time illustrates your commitment to continuous improvement.

What to Include in Your Portfolio

When building your portfolio, consider including:

- **Projects:**
  A selection of projects that demonstrate different aspects of your Ruby skills. This might include web applications, command-line tools, libraries, or automation scripts.

- **Case Studies:**
  Detailed write-ups of projects where you explain the challenges you faced, how you solved them, and what technologies you used.

This narrative can be especially compelling for potential employers.

- **Code Samples:**
  Clean, well-documented code hosted on platforms like GitHub. Ensure that your code is easy to read and highlights best practices.

- **Testimonials or References:**
  Feedback from colleagues, mentors, or clients that attest to your skills and professionalism.

Real-World Analogy:
Think of your portfolio as a digital resume or a personal museum. It's a curated collection of your best work that tells the story of your journey as a developer.

2.4 Theoretical Foundations Behind Professional Growth

Professional growth is a multifaceted pursuit that encompasses not only technical proficiency but also soft skills, networking, and the ability to adapt to new challenges. Here are some guiding principles:

- **Self-Reflection:**
  Regularly evaluate your strengths and areas for improvement.

- **Goal Setting:**
  Define short-term and long-term objectives for your learning and career development.

- **Mentorship:**
  Seek guidance from experienced developers and, in turn, mentor those who are starting out.

- **Community Involvement:**
  Contribute to open-source projects, write blog posts, or speak at local meetups to share your knowledge and build your reputation.

Using a Growth Mindset

Adopting a growth mindset means viewing challenges as opportunities to learn rather than as obstacles. This mindset is critical for professional development because it encourages experimentation, resilience, and continuous learning.

Analogy:
Consider a mountain climber who views each setback not as a failure but as a chance to learn and improve their technique. Similarly, every bug you encounter or new tool you learn is a stepping stone to becoming a better developer.

2.5 Recap of Core Theoretical Concepts

This section has provided an in-depth exploration of the theoretical concepts that underpin your next steps as a Ruby developer:

- **Community and Networking:**
  The importance of joining the Ruby community and how networking can open doors to mentorship and opportunities.

- **Continuing Education:**
  Why lifelong learning is critical and a curated list of resources to help you stay current.

- **Building Your Portfolio:**
  The value of a portfolio in demonstrating your skills and professional growth.

- **Professional Growth Mindset:**
  How setting goals, reflecting on your progress, and seeking mentorship can accelerate your career.

3. Tools and Setup

While this chapter is largely conceptual, having the right tools and environment to implement these ideas is crucial. In this section, we outline the essential tools and platforms you need to get started on your professional development journey.

3.1 Essential Software and Platforms

To build your portfolio and continue your education, ensure you have:

- **Ruby Interpreter:** The latest stable version installed.

- **Git and GitHub:** For version control and hosting your portfolio projects.

- **Text Editor/IDE:** Visual Studio Code or RubyMine for writing and editing code.

- **Project Management Tools:** Tools like Trello or Asana to keep track of your learning goals and project progress.

- **Portfolio Website Builders:** Platforms such as Jekyll (which works seamlessly with GitHub Pages) or WordPress to create an online portfolio.

3.2 Setting Up Your Development Environment

Follow these steps to set up an environment that supports your continuous learning and portfolio development:

1. **Install Ruby:**
   Use RVM or rbenv to install and manage Ruby versions. Verify with:

```bash
ruby -v
```

2. **Install Git:**
   Download and install Git, then configure your GitHub account:

```bash
git config --global user.name "Your Name"
git config --global user.email
"youremail@example.com"
```

3. **Select an Editor:**
   Download and configure Visual Studio Code or RubyMine with Ruby extensions.

4. **Create a GitHub Account:**
   Host your projects publicly or privately to showcase your work.

5. **Set Up a Portfolio Repository:**
   Create a new repository (e.g., portfolio) to host your project code and documentation.

3.3 Tools for Continuous Learning

Make use of additional tools that support learning:

- **RSS Readers:**
  Use tools like Feedly to subscribe to Ruby blogs and news sites.

- **Online Learning Platforms:**
  Bookmark sites like Codecademy, Udemy, and RubyMonk.

- **Community Tools:**
  Join Slack channels or Discord servers dedicated to Ruby developers.

3.4 Organizing Your Portfolio

Your portfolio should be well-structured, highlighting your best work. Consider the following structure for your online portfolio:

- **Homepage:**
  An introduction that summarizes your skills, experience, and interests.

- **Projects Section:**
  Detailed case studies and code samples for each project. Include screenshots, links to live demos, and GitHub repositories.

- **Blog or Articles:**
  Write about your experiences, lessons learned, or tutorials you've created.

- **Contact Information:**
  Provide a way for potential employers or collaborators to reach you.

3.5 Summary of Tools and Setup

In this section, we reviewed the essential software and platforms needed for your professional development. Setting up a robust development environment, organizing your projects with Git, and building a portfolio website are critical steps for showcasing your skills and advancing your career as a Ruby developer.

4. Hands-on Examples & Projects

This section provides practical examples and projects that demonstrate how to apply the concepts discussed in this chapter. These projects range from community engagement to building your portfolio, each designed to be engaging and actionable.

4.1 Example 1: Joining the Ruby Community

Project: "Community Engagement Tracker"

Develop a small Ruby script that helps you track community events, blog posts, and forum discussions. This script can fetch data from RSS feeds and display upcoming meetups.

1. **Create a File:**
   Name it community_tracker.rb.

2. **Write the Code:**

```ruby
require 'rss'
require 'open-uri'
require 'date'

# Define an array of RSS feed URLs from popular Ruby
community sources
rss_feeds = [

  "https://www.ruby-forum.com/index.rss",

  "https://rubyweekly.com/issues.rss"

]


rss_feeds.each do |feed_url|
  open(feed_url) do |rss|
    feed = RSS::Parser.parse(rss)
    puts "Feed: #{feed.channel.title}"
    feed.items.each do |item|
      pub_date = Date.parse(item.pubDate.to_s)
      if pub_date >= Date.today
```

```
    puts "Upcoming Event/Article: #{item.title}
(#{pub_date})"
    end
  end
  puts "-" * 40
 end
end
```

3. **Explanation:**

   o   This script uses Ruby's rss library to parse **RSS** feeds from community sites.

   o   It displays upcoming events or posts with publication dates on or after today.

   o   You can expand this script by integrating additional feeds or sending notifications.

4. **Exercise:**
   Modify the script to save the output to a file or send an email notification for new events.

4.2 Example 2: Creating an Online Portfolio with Jekyll

Project: "Build Your Portfolio Website"

Jekyll is a static site generator that works well with GitHub Pages. This project will guide you through setting up a simple portfolio website.

1. **Install Jekyll and Bundler:**

```bash

gem install jekyll bundler
```

2. **Create a New Jekyll Site:**

```bash

jekyll new portfolio
cd portfolio
bundle exec jekyll serve
```

3. **Customize the Site:**

- o Edit _config.yml to set your site's title, description, and author.

- o Create a new page called projects.md in the root directory:

markdown

```
---
layout: page
title: "Projects"
permalink: /projects/
---
```

My Projects

Here are some of my projects:

- **Inventory Management System:** A Ruby on Rails application for manufacturing.

- **Patient Management System:** A secure Ruby on Rails system for healthcare.

- **Shipment Tracker:** A Sinatra-based application for logistics.

4. **Deploy Your Site:**

- o Push your repository to GitHub and enable GitHub Pages.

- o Share your portfolio link on your resume and social media.

4.3 Example 3: Documenting Your Projects

Project: "Case Study Write-Up Template"

Develop a template for documenting your projects as case studies. This template can be used in your portfolio to describe each project in detail.

1. **Create a Markdown File:**
   Name it case_study_template.md.

2. **Write the Template:**

```markdown

# Project Title

## Overview
Brief description of the project, its purpose, and
the problem it solves.

## Technologies Used
- Ruby
- Ruby on Rails / Sinatra
- PostgreSQL / SQLite
- [Other Tools]
```

```
## Key Features
- Feature 1: [Description]
- Feature 2: [Description]
- Feature 3: [Description]

## Challenges and Solutions
Describe common challenges faced during development
and how you overcame them.

## Outcome and Impact
Explain how the project improved processes or solved
real-world problems.

## Lessons Learned
Reflect on what you learned and how it contributed to
your professional growth.
```

3. **Explanation:**

   o This template provides a consistent format for writing detailed case studies.

   o Include screenshots, code snippets, and diagrams where applicable.

   o Use this template to document each project in your portfolio.

4.4 Example 4: Tracking Your Professional Development

Project: "Learning Journal"

Maintain a learning journal using a simple Ruby script that logs your learning activities, courses completed, and meetups attended.

1. **Create a File:**
   Name it learning_journal.rb.

2. **Write the Code:**

```ruby
require 'csv'
require 'date'
```

```ruby
# Define the CSV file path
file_path = "learning_journal.csv"

# Check if the file exists; if not, create it with
headers
unless File.exist?(file_path)
  CSV.open(file_path, "w") do |csv|
    csv << ["Date", "Activity", "Resources", "Notes"]
  end
end

# Function to add an entry to the journal
def add_entry(file_path, activity, resources, notes)
  CSV.open(file_path, "a") do |csv|
    csv << [Date.today.to_s, activity, resources,
notes]
  end
end

# Example entries
add_entry(file_path, "Attended Ruby Meetup",
"Meetup.com", "Learned about Rails 7 new features.")
add_entry(file_path, "Completed Online Course",
"Codecademy Ruby Track", "Revisited basic syntax and
OOP principles.")

# Display the journal
puts "Learning Journal:"
CSV.foreach(file_path, headers: true) do |row|
  puts "#{row['Date']} - #{row['Activity']}:
#{row['Notes']}"
end
```

3. **Explanation:**

   o This script creates and maintains a CSV file that logs your learning activities.

   o The journal can be expanded by integrating with online services or even a simple web interface.

   o It provides a practical way to track your progress and reflect on your growth.

	A	B	C	D
1	**Name**	**Age**	**City**	**Occupation**
2	John Smith	35	New York	Engineer
3	Mary Johnson	28	Los Angeles	Designer
4	Michael Williams	40	Chicago	Teacher
5	Patricia Brown	52	Houston	Nurse
6	James Jones	24	Phoenix	Developer
7	Linda Garcia	30	Philadelphia	Manager
8	Robert Miller	45	San Antonio	Salesperson
9	Elizabeth Wilson	38	San Diego	Consultant
10	David Moore	22	Dallas	Student
11	Jennifer Taylor	31	New York	Writer

4.5 Recap of Hands-on Projects

The hands-on examples in this section have provided you with practical projects that support your continuous learning and portfolio building:

- A community engagement tracker that aggregates Ruby-related RSS feeds.

- An online portfolio website built with Jekyll and deployed via GitHub Pages.

- A case study template for documenting your projects.

- A learning journal script to track your professional development.

Each project is designed to be easily expandable and adaptable to your needs, helping you document and share your journey as a Ruby developer.

5. Advanced Techniques & Optimization

While the focus of this chapter is on next steps and resources, it is also important to consider advanced techniques that can optimize your ongoing learning and portfolio management efforts.

5.1 Optimizing Your Learning Workflow

Automation and Task Management

Automate repetitive tasks to free up time for learning. Tools like Rake or custom Ruby scripts can automate portfolio updates, blog posts, or data collection from community sources.

Example:

```ruby

# A simple Rake task to update your portfolio README
with latest project summaries
desc "Update portfolio summary"
task :update_portfolio do
  # Your code to pull the latest project data and
update a README file
  puts "Portfolio updated!"
end
```

Continuous Integration for Your Projects

Implement continuous integration (CI) pipelines for your portfolio projects. Use platforms like GitHub Actions or Travis CI to automatically run tests and deploy your projects.

Example:
A GitHub Actions workflow file (.github/workflows/ci.yml) can run your test suite every time you push new code.

5.2 Advanced Organization of Learning Resources

Creating a Personal Wiki

Organize your learning materials, notes, and resources in a personal wiki. Tools like Jekyll (again) or even Notion can serve as centralized repositories for your knowledge.

Using Version Control for Documentation

Keep your learning journal, case studies, and project write-ups under version control. This not only tracks changes but also demonstrates your commitment to continuous improvement.

5.3 Best Practices for Portfolio Optimization

Showcasing Diverse Skills

Ensure your portfolio highlights a range of skills—from simple scripts and web applications to more complex projects like API integrations or background job processing. Balance quality and quantity by carefully selecting projects that best represent your expertise.

Interactive Demos and Live Projects

Whenever possible, host interactive demos of your projects. Services like Heroku or GitHub Pages can allow potential employers to try out your applications directly.

Writing Detailed Documentation

Write clear documentation for each project in your portfolio. Include:

- An overview of the project.
- Key challenges and solutions.
- Technology stack and code samples.
- Lessons learned and future improvements.

5.4 Scaling Your Learning and Professional Development

Setting SMART Goals

Set Specific, Measurable, Achievable, Relevant, and Time-bound (SMART) goals for your continuous learning. For example, aim to complete one online course per month or contribute to an open-source project every quarter.

Tracking Progress and Adjusting Plans

Regularly review your progress, update your portfolio, and refine your learning strategies. Use tools like Trello or Asana to keep track of your learning objectives, projects, and milestones.

[Image Placeholder: Flowchart showing a goal-setting and progress tracking cycle]

5.5 Recap of Advanced Techniques & Optimization

In this section, we explored advanced methods to optimize your ongoing learning and portfolio management:

- Automating repetitive tasks to streamline your workflow.

- Implementing CI/CD pipelines to maintain high-quality projects.

- Organizing your learning resources effectively.

- Best practices for curating and presenting your portfolio.

- Setting and tracking SMART goals for professional growth.

These techniques are meant to help you not only build a better portfolio but also to maintain an efficient, productive learning process that keeps your skills current and your projects polished.

6. Troubleshooting and Problem-Solving

As you pursue continuous professional development and build your portfolio, you will inevitably encounter challenges—whether in organizing your projects, integrating new tools, or managing your time effectively. This section outlines common issues and provides troubleshooting strategies to help you overcome them.

6.1 Common Challenges in Continuing Education and Portfolio Building

Overwhelmed by Information

- **Symptom:** Feeling overloaded by the vast amount of learning resources available.

- **Solution:** Curate a focused list of resources and set aside dedicated time for learning. Use tools like **RSS** readers or bookmarking services to manage content.

Difficulty Staying Motivated

- **Symptom:** Losing momentum after initial enthusiasm.

- **Solution:** Set achievable goals, join community challenges, and celebrate small victories. Engage with peers to share your progress and get feedback.

Portfolio Maintenance Issues

- **Symptom:** Outdated projects or incomplete documentation.

- **Solution:** Schedule regular portfolio updates, review feedback, and refactor projects periodically. Automate parts of your workflow with scripts or CI/CD tools.

6.2 Troubleshooting Strategies for Professional Growth

Isolating the Issue

Break down challenges into smaller, manageable tasks. For example, if you're struggling to update your portfolio, focus first on organizing your projects into categories, then work on detailed case studies for each project.

Leveraging Community Resources

Use online forums, Slack channels, or local meetups to ask questions and share challenges. Often, someone else has encountered the same issue and can offer a solution.

Reflecting on Feedback

Constructively analyze feedback from mentors, peers, or portfolio visitors. Use this input to guide your next steps and continuously improve your work.

6.3 Before-and-After Examples

Consider a scenario where a developer's portfolio is cluttered and unfocused:

- **Before:** A portfolio with numerous unfinished projects, inconsistent documentation, and little context.

- **After:** A well-organized portfolio with clearly defined sections for projects, detailed case studies, and a professional design that highlights your skills.

By comparing these examples, you can identify specific areas for improvement and implement changes gradually.

6.4 Tools for Troubleshooting

- **Project Management Software:** Use Trello or Asana to break down tasks and track progress.

- **Version Control:** Regularly commit changes to GitHub to document improvements over time.

- **Online Communities:** Seek help on Stack Overflow, Reddit's r/ruby, or local meetups when stuck.

- **Self-Reflection Journals:** Maintain a journal (digital or physical) to document challenges and solutions.

6.5 Recap of Troubleshooting and Problem-Solving Techniques

Effective troubleshooting and problem-solving are essential to your professional development:

- Identify and isolate challenges by breaking them down into manageable parts.

- Leverage community support and online resources.

- Use feedback to refine your work and continuously update your portfolio.

- Employ project management tools to stay organized and motivated.

These strategies will help you maintain momentum in your continuous learning journey and ensure that your portfolio remains a strong representation of your skills and achievements.

7. Conclusion & Next Steps

As we conclude this chapter on Next Steps and Resources, it's time to reflect on what you've learned and outline a clear path forward for your professional development as a Ruby developer.

7.1 Summary of Main Points

- **Community and Continuing Education:**
  We explored how engaging with the Ruby community—through forums, local meetups, and online platforms—can significantly enhance your learning and career opportunities.

- **Further Learning:**
  A curated list of books, courses, and online resources was

provided to help you deepen your Ruby expertise and expand your technical horizons.

- **Building Your Portfolio:**
  Detailed advice was given on how to create a professional portfolio that showcases your projects, case studies, and overall growth as a developer.

- **Advanced Techniques:**
  We discussed methods to optimize your learning workflow, automate routine tasks, and set SMART goals for continuous improvement.

- **Troubleshooting and Problem-Solving:**
  Strategies were outlined to help you tackle common challenges, manage information overload, and stay motivated on your learning journey.

7.2 Next Steps for Your Professional Journey

Now that you have a roadmap for continuous learning and portfolio development, here are some actionable next steps:

- **Join the Community:**
  Sign up for a local Ruby meetup or join an online community forum. Engage actively by asking questions and sharing your progress.

- **Set Learning Goals:**
  Define clear, achievable goals for the next three to six months. Whether it's mastering a new framework or contributing to an open-source project, setting goals will keep you focused.

- **Build and Update Your Portfolio:**
  Start by documenting your existing projects using the case study template provided. Gradually expand your portfolio by adding new projects, detailed write-ups, and interactive demos.

- **Invest in Further Education:**
  Enroll in an online course, read one of the recommended books, or subscribe to a Ruby newsletter. Consistent, structured learning will ensure your skills remain current.

- **Reflect and Iterate:**
  Regularly review your progress. What worked well? What challenges did you encounter? Use this reflection to iterate on your learning and portfolio strategies.

7.3 Additional Resources and Where to Find Them

To continue your journey, refer to these resources:

- **Ruby Community Forums:**
  - Stack Overflow
  - Reddit's r/ruby
  - Ruby Forum

- **Meetups and Conferences:**
  - Meetup.com (search for Ruby groups)
  - RailsConf
  - RubyConf

- **Books:**
  - *Programming Ruby (The Pickaxe Book)*
  - *Practical Object-Oriented Design in Ruby* by Sandi Metz
  - *Eloquent Ruby* by Russ Olsen

- **Online Courses and Tutorials:**
  - Codecademy's Ruby Track
  - Udemy and Coursera courses on Ruby and Rails
  - RubyMonk

- **Portfolio Platforms:**
  - GitHub for code hosting and version control
  - GitHub Pages or Jekyll for portfolio website deployment

   o   WordPress for dynamic portfolio websites

7.4 Final Thoughts and Reflection

Your journey as a Ruby developer is just beginning. Every project you complete, every community event you attend, and every new skill you learn contributes to your growth as a professional. The key is to remain curious, stay engaged with the community, and always be willing to learn and adapt. Your portfolio is not just a collection of code—it's a reflection of your passion, creativity, and perseverance.

As you move forward:

- Embrace opportunities for collaboration and mentorship.

- Regularly update your portfolio to reflect your latest accomplishments.

- Challenge yourself with new projects that push your limits.

- Stay connected to the broader Ruby community and contribute back where you can.

Remember, the world of technology is always evolving. By committing to continuous education and proactive career development, you will not only keep pace with industry trends but also position yourself as a leader in the Ruby community.

Chapter 8: Wrap-Up: Review, Reflection, and Encouragement for Future Projects

1. Introduction

In every learning journey, there comes a moment to pause, reflect, and consolidate the progress you've made. This chapter serves as that critical wrap-up for your Ruby development guide. Here, we review the key concepts, techniques, and projects you've worked on throughout the guide, and we provide actionable suggestions for small projects you can tackle to reinforce your skills. We also offer encouragement and strategies for taking your Ruby programming to the next level by applying what you've learned to build your own applications with confidence.

The Significance of Reviewing and Reflecting

Why is it important to review what you've learned? In programming—and in life—reflection allows you to reinforce knowledge, identify areas for improvement, and build a solid foundation for future growth. By revisiting core concepts and examining how they interconnect, you not only cement your understanding but also begin to see how these pieces form a cohesive framework for building complex applications.

Think of this chapter as the "cool-down" after a strenuous workout. After pushing your limits and learning new techniques, you need time to stretch, reflect, and plan your next session. Reviewing your work, analyzing what went well, and pinpointing what could be improved is essential to continuous improvement. Whether you're a beginner, a seasoned professional, or a passionate hobbyist, taking stock of your progress is a crucial step in becoming a confident and capable Ruby developer.

Key Concepts and Terminology

Before diving deeper, let's clarify some important terms that will recur in this chapter:

- **Review:** A systematic examination of the material you've covered, highlighting key concepts and their applications.

- **Reflection:** The process of evaluating your learning experiences, successes, and challenges to guide future growth.

- **Small Projects:** Manageable coding exercises or mini-applications that reinforce core skills.

- **Portfolio:** A curated collection of projects and case studies that showcase your skills and achievements.

- **Future Projects:** New challenges that build upon your current knowledge and push your creative boundaries.

Setting the Tone for a New Chapter

This chapter is written in a professional yet encouraging tone. We aim to provide a clear, detailed summary of the guide's content while inspiring you to take the next step. The narrative is structured to be engaging and accessible—whether you're reviewing the basics or looking for advanced ideas for your next project, you'll find practical advice that resonates with your level of experience.

Throughout this chapter, you'll find examples, reflective questions, and project ideas that are designed to be both informative and actionable. Visual aids such as diagrams and flowcharts are suggested at key points (placeholders indicate where these visuals would be inserted in a fully published version) to help you visualize the connections between different concepts.

By the end of this chapter, you should have a thorough review of the material, a set of new project ideas to reinforce your skills, and a clear, actionable plan to continue your growth as a Ruby developer. Let's now move into the core concepts and theory behind effective review and reflection.

2. Core Concepts and Theory

This section reviews the theoretical underpinnings of the Ruby guide you've followed. It connects the dots between the various topics you have learned—from basic syntax and object-oriented programming to advanced web applications and testing—and demonstrates how they form a cohesive whole. We also use real-world analogies to make abstract ideas tangible.

2.1 Revisiting Ruby Fundamentals

Throughout this guide, you learned the core constructs of Ruby, such as:

- **Variables, Strings, and Numbers:** The basic building blocks of any program.

- **Control Structures:** Conditionals and loops that control the flow of execution.

- **Object-Oriented Programming:** How to create classes, objects, methods, and attributes to structure your code.

- **Error Handling and Debugging:** Techniques for managing exceptions and diagnosing problems in your code.

- **Web Application Development:** Using frameworks like Ruby on Rails and Sinatra to build robust applications.

- **Testing:** Ensuring your code works as expected with frameworks such as RSpec.

Imagine each of these topics as pieces of a puzzle. Individually, they are useful and interesting; together, they create a complete picture of what it means to be a proficient Ruby developer. Revisiting these fundamentals is like reviewing the blueprint of a building—you understand not only what each component does but also how they interconnect to form a stable structure.

2.2 The Importance of Hands-on Practice

One of the strongest themes of this guide has been the emphasis on practical, hands-on projects. You've built applications ranging from a simple "Hello, World!" script to complex web apps like a Task Manager. Each project was designed to reinforce the theoretical concepts and give you real-world experience in problem-solving.

Real-World Analogy:
Consider learning to drive. You read about the rules of the road and study the car's mechanics, but nothing replaces the experience of actually driving. Similarly, working on projects helps you internalize programming concepts and prepares you for the challenges of building production-grade applications.

2.3 Reflection as a Learning Tool

Reflection is a critical component of mastery. When you look back at what you've learned, you can identify patterns, recognize mistakes, and celebrate improvements. Here are some reflective questions you might ask yourself:

- Which concepts were most challenging, and how did I overcome them?

- How do the projects I built apply to real-world problems?

- What skills do I feel most confident in, and where do I still need improvement?

- How can I integrate these new skills into my professional work or personal projects?

Taking the time to answer these questions deepens your understanding and helps guide your next steps.

2.4 Professional Growth Through Continuous Learning

The technology field is in constant flux. Embracing a mindset of continuous improvement is key to staying relevant. The guide has introduced you to the importance of community involvement, further education, and maintaining a robust portfolio. These elements are all interconnected:

- **Community:** Sharing and discussing ideas with peers reinforces learning.

- **Further Education:** Books, courses, and tutorials expand your knowledge.

- **Portfolio:** Documenting your work not only showcases your skills but also serves as a record of your growth.

Analogy:
Think of your career as a journey on a long road. Every project, every meeting, every course is a milestone that builds your experience and propels you forward. By continuously learning and reflecting, you ensure that your journey is both progressive and fulfilling.

2.5 Summarizing the Core Theoretical Concepts

To summarize, this review covers:

- **Revisiting Fundamental Concepts:** A look back at the key elements of Ruby programming.

- **The Value of Hands-on Practice:** Understanding that real-world application is the best teacher.

- **Reflection as a Key to Mastery:** Recognizing how introspection helps refine your skills.

- **Continuous Professional Growth:** Emphasizing the importance of community, education, and portfolio building for long-term success.

With these theoretical concepts firmly in place, it's time to look at the tools and environment you need to continue building your skills and documenting your progress.

3. Tools and Setup

While much of this chapter is conceptual, having the right tools to support your ongoing learning and portfolio development is crucial. This section outlines the software, platforms, and strategies you need to set up a productive environment for continuous improvement.

3.1 Essential Software and Platforms

For your journey as a Ruby developer and for building a professional portfolio, you should have:

- **Ruby Interpreter:** Install the latest stable version of Ruby using RVM or rbenv.

- **Git and GitHub:** Use Git for version control and GitHub to host your code and portfolio projects.

- **Text Editor/IDE:** Visual Studio Code or RubyMine, with Ruby extensions for code highlighting, linting, and debugging.

- **Static Site Generators:** Tools like Jekyll to build portfolio websites, especially useful for GitHub Pages.

- **Project Management Tools:** Applications like Trello or Asana to track learning goals and project progress.

- **Learning Platforms:** Websites such as Codecademy, RubyMonk, or Udemy to continue your education.

3.2 Setting Up Your Development Environment

Follow these steps to create an environment that supports continuous learning and portfolio development:

1. **Install Ruby:**

bash

```
\curl -sSL https://get.rvm.io | bash -s stable
rvm install ruby
```

Verify your installation:

bash

```
ruby -v
```

2. **Install Git:** Download Git from git-scm.com and configure your user details:

bash

```
git config --global user.name "Your Name"
git config --global user.email "you@example.com"
```

3. **Set Up Your Editor:** Install Visual Studio Code or RubyMine and add Ruby extensions. Customize your settings for a comfortable coding experience.

4. **Create a GitHub Account and Repository:** Sign up at GitHub, create a new repository (e.g., portfolio), and clone it to your local machine:

```bash
```

```
git clone
https://github.com/yourusername/portfolio.git
```
Build a Static Portfolio Site: *Use Jekyll to create a simple portfolio:*
```bash
```

```
gem install jekyll bundler
jekyll new my_portfolio
cd my_portfolio
bundle exec jekyll serve
```
Access your portfolio at http://localhost:4000 and customize the content.

3.3 Organizing Your Projects and Documentation

An organized environment is key to maintaining clarity:

- **Folder Structure:**
  Organize your projects by topic (e.g., web apps, utilities, case studies) and maintain a dedicated folder for your portfolio.

- **Documentation:**
  Write clear README files for each project. Use Markdown to format your documentation, and include sections like Overview, Features, Technologies, and Lessons Learned.

- **Version Control:**
  Commit your changes regularly and use Git branches to manage experimental features or updates.

3.4 Tools for Ongoing Learning

To support your continuous education:

- **RSS Readers:**
  Use Feedly to subscribe to Ruby blogs, newsletters, and industry news.

- **Bookmark Managers:**
  Tools like Pocket or Evernote can help you organize and revisit useful articles and tutorials.

- **Community Platforms:**
  Join Slack channels, Discord servers, and forums dedicated to Ruby and Rails.

3.5 Summary of Tools and Setup

This section has outlined the essential tools and configuration steps to create an environment conducive to continuous learning and professional portfolio development. With Ruby, Git, a reliable editor, and platforms for documentation and networking, you're well-equipped to implement the strategies discussed in this chapter.

---

4. Hands-on Examples & Projects

In this section, we provide practical, hands-on projects that tie together the concepts of review, reflection, and professional development. These projects are designed to reinforce your learning and help you build a portfolio that showcases your abilities.

4.1 Example 1: Mini-Projects for Reinforcement

Project: "Code Review Challenge"

Build a small Ruby script that quizzes you on key concepts from the guide. This exercise not only reinforces your knowledge but also highlights areas for further study.

1. **Create a File:**
   Name it code_review_challenge.rb.

2. Write the Code:

ruby

```ruby
# code_review_challenge.rb
QUESTIONS = {
  "What is a Ruby gem?" => "A packaged library or
application",
  "What does 'DRY' stand for?" => "Don't Repeat
Yourself",
  "Name one popular Ruby web framework." => "Ruby on
Rails"
}

def start_quiz
  score = 0
  QUESTIONS.each do |question, answer|
    puts question
    print "Your answer: "
    user_answer = gets.chomp
    if user_answer.downcase.include?(answer.downcase)
      puts "Correct!"
      score += 1
    else
      puts "Incorrect. The correct answer is:
#{answer}."
    end
    puts "-" * 40
  end
  puts "Your final score is
#{score}/#{QUESTIONS.size}"
end
```

start_quiz

3. Explanation:

- This script uses a hash to store questions and answers.

- It iterates through each question, checks your response, and provides immediate feedback.

- Use this challenge to review key concepts and identify areas that need further study.

4. **Exercise:**
   Expand the challenge by adding more questions or incorporating topics from advanced sections of the guide.

4.2 Example 2: Building a Personal Portfolio Website

Project: "My Ruby Portfolio"

Develop a portfolio website using Jekyll that displays your projects, case studies, and learning journey. This project not only demonstrates your Ruby skills but also serves as a professional showcase.

1. **Set Up a New Jekyll Site:**

bash

```
jekyll new my_portfolio
cd my_portfolio
bundle exec jekyll serve
```

2. **Customize the Site:**

   o Edit _config.yml to set your site's title, description, and author.

   o Create a new Markdown file projects.md with details of your projects:

markdown

```
---
layout: page
title: "Projects"
permalink: /projects/
---


## My Projects


- **Code Review Challenge:** A Ruby script to test your knowledge.

- **Inventory Management System:** A Rails app for manufacturing.
```

- **Patient Management System:** A secure application for healthcare.

- **Shipment Tracker:** A Sinatra app for logistics.

3. **Deploy Your Site:**
   Push your repository to GitHub and set up GitHub Pages to host your portfolio online.

4. **Explanation:**

   o This project helps you create a dynamic, professional portfolio.

   o It showcases your projects and provides context for your work through case studies and reflective write-ups.

5. **Exercise:**
   Enhance your portfolio by adding a blog section where you write about your learning experiences and challenges.

4.3 Example 3: Documenting Your Learning Journey

Project: "Learning Journal"

Create a learning journal that logs your progress, courses completed, and meetups attended. This journal can be a simple Ruby script that writes entries to a CSV file or a full-featured web app.

1. **Create a File:**
   Name it learning_journal.rb.

2. **Write the Code:**

```ruby
require 'csv'
require 'date'

FILE_PATH = "learning_journal.csv"

# Create the CSV file with headers if it does not
exist
unless File.exist?(FILE_PATH)
  CSV.open(FILE_PATH, "w") do |csv|
```

```
      csv << ["Date", "Activity", "Resource",
"Reflection"]
    end
end

def add_entry(activity, resource, reflection)
  CSV.open(FILE_PATH, "a") do |csv|
    csv << [Date.today.to_s, activity, resource,
reflection]
  end
end

# Example entries
add_entry("Completed RubyMonk challenge", "RubyMonk",
"Improved my understanding of control structures.")
add_entry("Attended local Ruby meetup", "Meetup.com",
"Learned about best practices in Rails development.")

puts "Learning Journal Entries:"
CSV.foreach(FILE_PATH, headers: true) do |row|
  puts "#{row['Date']}: #{row['Activity']} -
#{row['Reflection']}"
end
```

3. **Explanation:**

   o   This script logs learning activities in a CSV file.

   o   It can be extended to include more features, such as emailing weekly summaries or integrating with a web dashboard.

4. **Exercise:**
   Enhance the script to allow for interactive input from the command line and save the entries dynamically.

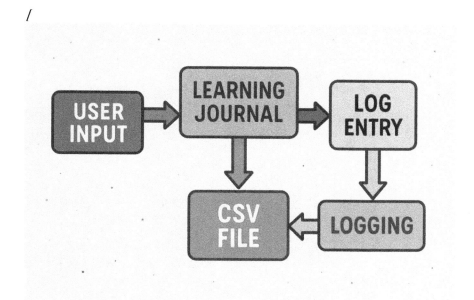

4.4 Example 4: Creating Case Studies for Your Projects

Project: "Case Study Template Generator"

Develop a simple tool that helps you generate case study templates for documenting your projects. This template can then be refined and added to your portfolio.

1. **Create a File:**
   Name it case_study_template.rb.

2. **Write the Code:**

ruby

```ruby
# case_study_template.rb
TEMPLATE = <<~TEMPLATE
  # Project Title

  ## Overview
  Brief description of the project, its goals, and
the problem it addresses.
```

```
## Technologies Used
- Ruby
- Ruby on Rails / Sinatra
- Database: PostgreSQL / SQLite
- Additional Tools: [List any other technologies]

## Key Features
- Feature 1: [Description]
- Feature 2: [Description]
- Feature 3: [Description]

## Challenges and Solutions
Describe the challenges faced during development
and the strategies used to overcome them.

## Outcome and Impact
Explain the results of the project and its impact
on the problem domain.

## Lessons Learned
Reflect on the project's successes and areas for
improvement.
TEMPLATE
```

File.write("case_study_template.md", TEMPLATE)

puts "Case study template generated successfully as 'case_study_template.md'."

3. **Explanation:**

   o This script creates a Markdown file with a pre-formatted case study template.

   o Use this template for each project you wish to document in your portfolio.

4. **Exercise:**
   Customize the template further by adding sections for future enhancements or client testimonials.

4.5 Recap of Hands-on Projects

In this section, you explored several practical projects designed to reinforce your learning and build your professional portfolio:

- A **Code Review Challenge** script to quiz your knowledge.

- A **Portfolio Website** built with Jekyll to showcase your projects.

- A **Learning Journal** script to track your progress and reflections.

- A **Case Study Template Generator** to document your projects in detail.

Each project not only reinforces core concepts but also provides tangible outputs that you can use to demonstrate your expertise to potential employers or collaborators.

5. Advanced Techniques & Optimization

Although this chapter focuses on next steps and resources, it's important to touch on advanced techniques that can optimize your ongoing learning and portfolio management. Here, we briefly discuss strategies to streamline your workflow and maximize the impact of your projects.

5.1 Optimizing Your Learning Workflow

Automation Tools

Automate repetitive tasks such as updating your portfolio or sending reminders to add journal entries. Tools like Rake or custom Ruby scripts can handle these tasks, saving you time and energy.

Continuous Integration for Your Projects

Implement CI/CD pipelines for your portfolio projects. Use GitHub Actions or Travis CI to run tests automatically whenever you push updates. This ensures your projects remain robust and up to date.

Example:
A GitHub Actions workflow that automatically tests your Ruby projects on every commit.

5.2 Advanced Organization of Resources

Creating a Central Repository

Maintain a central repository (or personal wiki) where you store all your learning materials, notes, and resources. This repository should be easily searchable and regularly updated.

Using Version Control for Documentation

Keep your project documentation, case studies, and learning journals under version control. This not only tracks your progress over time but also demonstrates your commitment to continuous improvement.

5.3 Best Practices for Portfolio Optimization

Showcasing a Variety of Skills

Your portfolio should reflect the breadth of your abilities. Include projects that highlight different aspects of Ruby—web applications, scripts, automation tools, and open-source contributions. Quality over quantity is key.

Interactive Demos and Live Examples

Where possible, host live demos of your projects. Use platforms like Heroku or GitHub Pages to deploy your applications, and link these demos in your portfolio.

Detailed Documentation

Ensure every project in your portfolio is accompanied by thorough documentation. This documentation should include an overview, technical details, challenges faced, solutions implemented, and lessons learned.

5.4 Recap of Advanced Techniques & Optimization

To summarize, the advanced techniques discussed here help you streamline your learning process and optimize your portfolio:

- Automate routine tasks and use CI/CD pipelines.

- Organize your learning resources in a central repository.

- Optimize your portfolio to showcase diverse projects with thorough documentation.

- Set and track **SMART** goals for continuous improvement.

6. Troubleshooting and Problem-Solving

Even the most well-organized plans can encounter obstacles. In this section, we provide strategies for troubleshooting common issues that arise in your ongoing learning and portfolio development efforts.

6.1 Common Challenges

Overwhelming Information

- **Issue:** Feeling overloaded by the sheer amount of available resources.

- **Solution:** Curate a focused list of high-quality sources and set aside dedicated time each week for learning.

Motivation Slumps

- **Issue:** Losing momentum after initial enthusiasm.

- **Solution:** Set small, achievable goals and track your progress in a learning journal. Celebrate every milestone.

Portfolio Maintenance

- **Issue:** Projects and documentation become outdated.

- **Solution:** Schedule periodic reviews of your portfolio and update projects as needed. Automate parts of this process where possible.

6.2 Effective Problem-Solving Strategies

Breaking Down Problems

When faced with a challenge—be it technical or organizational—break it down into smaller, manageable tasks. This makes the problem less daunting and allows you to tackle it step by step.

Leveraging Community Feedback

Use online forums and local meetups to seek advice when you're stuck. Sharing your challenges with the community can lead to new insights and solutions.

Iterative Improvement

Adopt an iterative approach to your portfolio and learning resources. Regularly reflect on what's working, adjust your strategies, and continuously refine your processes.

6.3 Before-and-After Examples

Consider a scenario where your portfolio was initially disorganized and lacked documentation:

- **Before:** Projects are scattered, and documentation is minimal or inconsistent.

- **After:** Projects are organized into clear categories, each with detailed case studies, interactive demos, and thorough documentation.

Reflect on these changes as examples of how iterative improvements can significantly enhance your professional presentation.

6.4 Tools to Assist in Troubleshooting

- **Project Management Software:** Tools like Trello or Asana help you break down tasks and monitor progress.

- **Version Control Systems:** Git not only tracks code changes but also helps you manage updates to your portfolio documentation.

- **Community Platforms:** Engage with online communities on Reddit, Stack Overflow, and local meetups for support and advice.

6.5 Summary of Troubleshooting Techniques

This section has outlined key strategies for overcoming challenges in your continuous learning journey:

- Identify and break down challenges into smaller tasks.

- Use community feedback and project management tools.

- Regularly review and update your portfolio and learning materials.

These troubleshooting strategies will help you maintain your momentum and ensure that your progress remains consistent over time.

---

7. Conclusion & Next Steps

In this final section, we wrap up the chapter by summarizing the key points, providing a roadmap for your future learning, and offering final words of encouragement to help you move forward with confidence.

7.1 Summary of Key Points

Throughout this chapter, we have explored:

- **Community and Continuing Education:**
  The importance of engaging with the Ruby community through forums, meetups, and online platforms, and how to leverage these networks for ongoing learning.

- **Further Learning Resources:**
  A curated list of books, courses, online tutorials, and newsletters that can help you build on the skills you've acquired.

- **Building Your Portfolio:**
  Practical advice on compiling projects, writing case studies, and organizing your work in a professional portfolio that highlights your growth and achievements.

- **Advanced Techniques for Optimization:**
  Strategies to streamline your learning workflow, automate
  repetitive tasks, and maintain an updated, high-quality portfolio.

- **Troubleshooting and Problem-Solving:**
  Methods to overcome common challenges, stay motivated, and
  continuously refine your approach to professional development.

7.2 Next Steps for Your Professional Journey

As you finish this guide, it's time to look ahead and plan your next steps.
Here are some actionable suggestions:

- **Join a Ruby Community:**
  Register for local meetups, join online forums, or subscribe to
  Ruby newsletters like Ruby Weekly. Engaging with peers will help
  you stay informed and inspired.

- **Set Clear Learning Goals:**
  Identify areas where you want to improve and set SMART
  (Specific, Measurable, Achievable, Relevant, Time-bound) goals.
  Whether it's learning a new framework, contributing to
  open-source projects, or mastering advanced Ruby techniques,
  clear goals keep you on track.

- **Develop New Projects:**
  Use the project ideas from this guide as a starting point. Tackle
  small projects that challenge you to apply what you've learned,
  then gradually increase the complexity. For instance, create a
  personal task manager, a blogging platform, or an API that
  integrates with external data sources.

- **Update Your Portfolio:**
  Document your projects and write detailed case studies. Use the
  templates and tools provided in this chapter to ensure your
  portfolio is comprehensive and professional. Remember, your
  portfolio is a living document that should evolve with your skills.

- **Keep Learning:**
  Continue taking online courses, reading books, and following
  industry trends. The technology landscape is always evolving, and
  continuous learning is key to staying ahead.

7.3 Additional Resources

To further support your journey, here is a list of valuable resources:

- **Community Forums:**
    - Stack Overflow
    - Reddit's r/ruby
    - Ruby Forum
- **Meetups and Conferences:**
    - Meetup.com (search for Ruby groups)
    - RailsConf
    - RubyConf
- **Books:**
    - *Programming Ruby (The Pickaxe Book)*
    - *Practical Object-Oriented Design in Ruby* by Sandi Metz
    - *Eloquent Ruby* by Russ Olsen
- **Online Courses:**
    - Codecademy's Ruby Track
    - Courses on Udemy and Coursera
    - RubyMonk and Pluralsight tutorials
- **Portfolio Platforms:**
    - GitHub for code hosting and version control
    - GitHub Pages or Jekyll for creating a portfolio website
    - WordPress for dynamic portfolio websites

7.4 Final Thoughts and Reflection

As you reach the end of this guide, take a moment to reflect on your journey. Consider the challenges you've overcome and the skills you've acquired. Every line of code you've written, every project you've built, and every problem you've solved has contributed to your growth as a developer. Your portfolio isn't just a collection of projects—it's a testament to your perseverance, creativity, and commitment to continuous improvement.

Looking ahead, remember:

- **Keep Experimenting:**
  Don't be afraid to try new ideas and push your boundaries. The best learning happens when you step out of your comfort zone.

- **Stay Engaged:**
  Actively participate in the Ruby community. Share your projects, ask questions, and offer help to others.

- **Reflect Regularly:**
  Use tools like learning journals or project retrospectives to evaluate your progress and adjust your strategies.

- **Celebrate Milestones:**
  Every project completed is a victory. Recognize your accomplishments, however small, and let them motivate you to tackle new challenges.

Your journey as a Ruby developer is ongoing. With the tools, resources, and insights provided in this guide, you are well-prepared to continue growing and making an impact—whether that's in your current job, a side project, or even a new startup. The world of Ruby is full of opportunities waiting to be explored, and now is the perfect time to take the next step.